LAND OF LIABILITY

A Guide for California Employers

Daniel Thompson, Esq.

Copyright © 2020 Daniel Thompson, Esq.

All rights reserved.

ISBN: 9798643555308

DEDICATION

To all California employers.

CONTENTS

	Acknowledgments	i
1	Land of Liability	1
2	Corporate Formation	6
3	Hiring	12
4	Independent Contractors	23
5	Wages	29
6	Meal and Rest Periods	41
7	Employee Handbooks	46
8	Record-Keeping Requirements	49
9	Leaves of Absence	52
10	Workplace Safety	62
11	Harassment	70
12	Discrimination	76
13	Whistleblowers	84
14	Wrongful Termination	90
15	Litigation	102

DISCLOSURE

The information contained in this book is for educational purposes only. It should not be construed as legal advice and the author does not intend to form an attorney-client relationship. Employment cases are determined on a case-by-case basis and, therefore, employers are encouraged to contact a qualified attorney for advice.

CHAPTER ONE
LAND OF LIABILITY

Ever since the Gold Rush of 1849, California has been labeled the Land of Opportunity – a place where hard work and a little luck could be rewarded by great wealth.

California has enjoyed a long history of creating successful industries such as entertainment, aerospace, wineries and Silicon Valley. For other industries, however, the California Dream is interrupted by California Reality – high taxes, mandatory insurance and suffocating regulations.

Each year, the Small Business and Entrepreneurial Council releases the "Small Business Policy Index," which ranks the states on policy measures and costs impacting small business and entrepreneurship. Unsurprisingly, California is routinely ranked as the worst state for small businesses.

The reasons for the low rankings include: high minimum wage, mandatory worker's compensation insurance, short-term disability insurance obligations, family leave regulations, energy costs, land use regulations and high start-up costs.

Despite the government-created difficulties that come from owning a small business, California maintains a large number of employers with fewer than 500 employees. According to the Small Business Administration's 2021 Small Business Profile, there were 4.2 million small businesses in California, representing a staggering 99.8% of all business entities in the state. These small businesses employed 48.8% of the California workforce, or roughly 7.3 million workers.

In other words, the vast majority of business entities are small businesses while the majority of employees are employed by large businesses – the largest of which is the State of California. This creates an inherent imbalance when determining the needs of California businesses.

The purpose of this book, however, is not to discuss the causes of California's business oppression. That would be far too political. Rather, this book seeks to assist employers by accepting the reality that California has become a Land of Liability.

This is not to say that opportunity no longer exists in California. On the contrary, California still maintains the largest consumer population in country. The potential for wealth is always present. California employers just have other obstacles to overcome in order to obtain success.

The goal of any business is to make a profit. In the most basic format, the formula for profit is simple:

Revenue – Expenses = Profit

However, as any business owner knows, this is an oversimplification. The real formula looks something like this:

Revenue – Expenses – Payroll – Insurance – Rent – Taxes – Loan Payments = Profit

Every time money is spent, profits decrease. However, these costs are all an anticipated part of business. After all, three eggs must be broken to make a three-egg omelette. What most businesses do not anticipate is liability.

Liability attacks profits on the backend. It is like someone demanding an egg after the omelette has been eaten. After the expense reports are complete and profits have been distributed, liability rears its ugly head and declares, "You did something wrong. Give me what you've earned."

There are many forms of business liability. For example, a slip and fall can trigger premises liability for personal injury. Failure to adhere to terms of an agreement will bring liability for breach of contract.

The type of liability discussed in this book arises from the employment relationship. In recent years, employment law has grown at an exponential rate due to the passage of new laws governing the employment relationship. Over time, the judiciary reviews these laws and determines the extent of their applicability.

Imagine a professional football game, before the game, the league creates a standard set of rules by which both teams must abide. The referees enforce those rules and determine the extent to which they are enforced. Now, imagine a scenario where the league can change the rules at any time and the referees did not enforce penalties until after the game.

As will be discussed in this book, the rule-changing analogy is one of many labilities faced by California employers. With so many changes in the law, many employers fall behind and become vulnerable to liability. A team may claim victory only to have the score reduced after the referee decides how the penalties will be enforced.

What this book seeks to do is provide businesses with practical information to discover and avoid liability. As with vehicles and health, prevention is better than treatment. It is better to know about liability before a lawsuit is filed. If a lawsuit has been filed, it is already too late.

An old Chinese proverb tells the story of a monk who carried two buckets across his shoulders each morning to retrieve water from a well. One bucket was new and the other had holes. One morning, the leaky bucket complained to the monk about never being fixed. The monk said to the bucket, "Look how barren the side of the road is where the perfect bucket passed over. Not even a blade of grass grows here. Now look at your side of the road. These beautiful flowers are here only because of the water you sprinkle on them every day. Your imperfection has brought benefits to people around you."

While this is a beautiful sentiment, it has no place in business. What good is a leaky bucket? Only a fool would break his back every morning to water someone else's flowers. In the case of litigation, the lost profits from leaks of liability will only benefit a trial lawyer.

This book will reveal common leaks in the employment relationship which, if properly fixed, will allow a business to keep its water and find prosperity in this Land of Liability.

CHAPTER TWO
CORPORATE FORMATION

Determining how a business entity will operate is the first important legal decision of any business owner. The two primary reasons for this are taxes and personal liability.

Whether the business is a partnership, corporation or limited liability corporation, it is important to realize that the legal entity, in many legal constructs, is considered a person.

Think about that for a moment.

The only other way to create a person is through the biological process of procreation. For a small fee, the law permits anyone to file corporate documents and create a living being in the eyes of the law. It has a name and an address. The business entity can own land. It can be taxed. It can die. The business entity can sue and be sued. It can be convicted of a crime. A business entity can even marry another business entity and create little baby business entities called subsidiaries.

Perhaps the most important benefit of this

unembodied person is that it can shield its owners, directors, shareholders and managers from liability. Unfortunately, instead of creating a separate and distinct entity, some owners treat their business as an extension of themselves. Owners create a type of corporate avatar that is nothing more than a manifestation of themselves into the world of business.

Here is an example:

George's wife loves throw pillows. George decides to start a business designing and distributing decorative throw pillows. His attorney recommends forming a corporation. George does so and names his wife as the only other shareholder. George and his wife begin using corporate funds to take family vacations under the guise that they are business trips to obtain design ideas. They also use business funds to furnish their house and test new products. Not surprisingly, the business fails. A creditor sues the corporation for failure to pay a business loan. When it is discovered that the corporation has no money, the creditor sues George and his wife as alter egos.

The Alter Ego Doctrine is used to the "pierce the corporate veil" and hold owners liable for the actions of the business entity. It applies when owners, such as George, do not respect the entity's separate identity. Common examples are when owners or shareholders:

- Use business assets as their own (e.g., withdraw corporate funds for personal use without treating such withdrawals as salaries or dividends);
- Fail to contribute capital, issue stock or

otherwise complete formation of the corporation;
- Commingle business funds with their personal funds; or
- Fail to observe corporate formalities (e.g., fail to regularly elect directors, appoint officers, hold board meetings and keep minutes or file corporate tax returns).

Even if a corporation is named after its owner, it is still a separate business entity. John Doe, Inc. is not John Doe. The separation must be respected. Failure to do so creates another pathway to liability. When the leaky bucket runs out of water, the creditor will be able to take water stored inside the house.

Here is the frightening thing about employment law: For certain offenses, the state of California has provided a statutory pathway to automatically pierce the corporate veil.

For example, Labor Code § 226.8 prohibits the willful misclassification of employees as independent contractors by any "person or employer." Liability even extends to any person who knowingly advises an employer to treat an individual as an independent contractor.

In October 2015, California passed the "A Fair Day's Pay Act," which expands liability for willful wage and hour violations to owners, directors, officers, and managing agents of the employer through Labor Code § 558.1. The federal Fair Labor Standards Act, has a similar provision and extends liability to "any person" acting in the employer's interest in dealing with employees (29 USC § 203(d)).

This is why knowing the law and avoiding liability is so critical. When business liability breaches the corporate veil, it puts personal assets at risk.

Oh, and on the issue of corporate formation, the state of California now requires that a publicly held corporation whose executive offices are located in California must have at least one female on its board of directors. No later than December 31, 2021, corporations are required to have a minimum number to two female directors if the corporation has five directors or three female directors if the corporation has six or more directors.

The violation of this law will carry a hefty fine as it provides that the Secretary of State may adopt regulations to implement this section and may impose the following penalties: (a) $100,000 for failure to timely file board member information with the Secretary of State; (b) $100,000 for a first violation; and (c) $300,000 for a second or subsequent violation.

With all that said, here is a brief overview of corporate formation. Even if the veil can be pierced, it is a good idea to have it in place. A bulletproof vest may not be able to stop all caliber bullets, but it will provide protection from a majority of them.

There are four basic choices for forming a business: sole proprietorship, partnership, corporation and limited liability company. Each one has its advantages and disadvantages, so consideration should be given to personnel needs and the needs of a particular type of business.

<u>Sole Proprietorship</u> - A sole proprietorship

permits an individual to own and operate a business. A sole proprietor has total control, receives all profits from and is responsible for taxes and liabilities of the business. If a sole proprietorship is formed with a name other than the individual's name (example: Don Juan de Taco Shop), the owner must file a Fictitious Business Name Statement with the county where the principal place of business is located.

<u>Partnership</u> - There are multiple types of partnerships. In a Limited Partnership, there must be at least one general partner that acts as the controlling partner and one limited partner whose liability is normally limited to the amount of control or participation of the limited partner. General partners of a Limited Partnership have unlimited personal liability for the partnership's debts and obligation.

General Partnerships must have two or more persons engaged in a business for profit. Except as otherwise provided by law, all partners are liable jointly and severally for all obligations of the partnership unless agreed by the claimant. Profits are taxed as personal income for the partners.

Limited Liability Partnerships ("LLP") engage in the practices of accountancy, law, architecture, engineering or land surveying, or provide services or facilities to a California registered LLP that practices public accountancy or law, or to a foreign LLP. An LLP is required to maintain certain levels of insurance as required by law.

<u>Corporation</u> - A Corporation is a legal entity which exists separately from its owners. While normally limiting the owners from personal liability, taxes are levied on the corporation as well as on the

shareholders. The sale of stocks or bonds can generate additional capital and the longevity of the corporation can continue past the death of the owners. Legal Counsel should be consulted regarding the variety of options available.

<u>Limited Liability Company (LLC)</u> - A Limited Liability Company offers liability protection similar to that of a corporation but is taxed differently. Domestic LLCs may be managed by one or more managers or one or more members. In addition to filing the applicable documents with the Secretary of State, an operating agreement among the members as to the affairs of the LLC and the conduct of its business is required. The LLC does not file the operating agreement with the Secretary of State but maintains it at the office where the LLC's records are kept.

When deciding on the best business formation, it is a good idea to seek the advice of a competent attorney and accountant.

CHAPTER THREE
HIRING

Hiring the right people is the key to business success. Hiring the right people in the wrong way can lead to liability.

While applicants for employment are afforded less protection than regular employees, they still enjoy a wide range of constitutional, statutory, and common-law rights. California has many laws governing what employers can and cannot say during the hiring process. The major areas of inquiry are addressed below.

<u>Discrimination</u>

The California Fair Employment and Housing Act (FEHA) makes it illegal for an employer to discriminate because of race, religious creed, color, national origin, ancestry, physical disability, mental disability, medical condition, genetic information, marital status, sex, gender, gender identity, gender expression, age, sexual orientation, or military and veteran status of any person. Gov. Code, § 12940, subd. (a).

These protected classes should be memorized by every employer. The long reach of FEHA will be discussed throughout this book, so there will be ample opportunity to do so.

In order to avoid the appearance of discrimination, employers should limit requests for information during the pre-employment process to those details essential to determining a person's qualifications to do the job. The following are some general guidelines that employers should know regarding the employment application process.

Name: An employer should never ask questions about an individual's name that require the applicant to disclose ancestry, national origin, race, religion or marital status, (i.e., asking for an applicant's "maiden" name, or asking questions about the origin of a name). However, it is acceptable to ask an applicant's name or previous name for purposes of checking their past work record.

Age: Unless age is a bona fide occupational qualification, it is not acceptable to ask questions that would otherwise reveal age, such as school attendance dates. However, it is acceptable to ask individuals to affirm that they meet legal age requirements during the application process, and to require proof of age after hire (i.e., asking if the applicant is over 18).

Sex: Asking an applicant to identify their sex is never acceptable, unless sex is a bona fide occupational qualification. The classic example is Victoria's Secret's prohibition against men modeling their newest women's undergarment collection.

Employers should never use proxies for sex, such as stating height or weight preferences unless they are a bona fide occupational qualification.

Race / Color: It is never acceptable to ask questions about an applicant's race or color. There is simply no reason for this sort of inquiry as race or color are never a bona fide occupational qualification.

Pregnancy / Breastfeeding / Fertility: Asking about pregnancy, breastfeeding, or fertility/childbirth is rarely acceptable. An employer cannot claim to hire nonpregnant women based on fears of danger to the fetus, fears of potential tort liability, assumptions and stereotypes about the employment characteristics of pregnant women such as their turnover rate, or customer preference.

Gender / Gender Identity / Gender Expression: Under California law, it is never acceptable to ask questions about an applicant's gender identity or expression. This includes questions about medical or surgical status or procedures. An employer may only ask about biological sex or gender if it is a bona fide occupational qualification.

Marital or Family Status: Generally, an employer may not ask questions regarding marital status or the age/number of children or dependents. However, an employer may ask if the applicant is related to any current employee if the employer has a policy of refusing to place a close relative under the direct supervision of another relative, or if the work involves potential conflicts of interests or other hazards increased by the familial relationship.

Disability / Medical Conditions: Employers may

ask if an applicant can perform essential job-related functions with or without accommodation. They can also inquire as to the medical history of applicants if it is directly related and pertinent to the position the applicant is applying for or directly related to a determination of whether the applicant would endanger his or her health or safety or the health or safety of others.

National Origin / Ancestry: It is permissible to ask employees regarding language ability in languages other than English, if relevant to the job. However, employers may not ask questions about nationality, ancestry, descent or parentage, or ask questions regarding how foreign language ability was acquired.

Physical Appearance: Employers may not require or request that applicants submit photographs with their applications or require a photograph after an interview but before hiring, unless there is a defensible business reason to do so (i.e. actor headshots). However, it is acceptable for an employer to make a statement that a photograph may be required after employment.

Citizenship: Many employers ask about citizenship out of concern for federal laws that prohibit hiring undocumented immigrant workers. However, non-citizens may still be authorized to work in the United States through a work visa. Therefore, the proper mode of questioning is to ask whether the applicant has "the legal right to work in the United States," as opposed to inquiring about citizenship. Employers should never ask questions about the birthplace of an applicant or the applicant's family.

Religion: An employer may not ask questions regarding an individual's religion or lack thereof, or about religious practice, affiliation, or religious holidays observed unless there is a bona fide occupational qualification. An employer may inquire into availability to work on weekends or evenings where reasonably related to normal business requirements.

Military Status: Military status is a little different. In general, employers should not request dates or nature of military service or veteran status. However, employers must permit applicants to include information about military service in the experience or skills section of the application if the applicant so desires.

Social Media: Labor Code § 980 prohibits an employer from asking an employee or applicant to provide access to his or her personal social media account or to disclose a personal social media password. In addition, an employer is prohibited from taking retaliatory action against an employee who refuses to comply with such a request. Exceptions are permitted when the employer needs the employee's username or password to access an employer-issued electronic device. An employer may also request personal social media access when conducting an investigation of employee misconduct as long as the information is reasonably believed to be relevant and is used solely for the investigation.

Ban the Box

Employers tend to disfavor hiring employees with a propensity for criminal activity. Most employers avoid this by asking about criminal history and performing background checks. However, the state of California has found it necessary to balance the rights of rehabilitated criminals against the rights of employers.

California's "Ban the Box" law prohibits most private and public employers from inquiring into or considering a job applicant's conviction history before a conditional offer of employment has been made. If an employer intends to withdraw a conditional offer based solely on the applicant's conviction history, it must first conduct an individualized assessment that considers: the nature and gravity of the offense or conduct; the time elapsed since the offense or conduct and completion of the sentence; and the nature of the job in question.

Employers cannot ask an applicant about arrests. With respect to convictions, most employers cannot ask about convictions which resulted in a referral to, and participation in, any pretrial or post-trial diversion program; have been judicially expunged, statutorily eradicated, dismissed after probation, or ordered sealed; or related to marijuana offenses that occurred two years prior to the application. It also does not apply to any position where an employer is required by another law to conduct background checks or restrict employment based on criminal history. Cal. Bus. & Prof. Code § 7583.9.

After offering a job, employers are allowed to conduct a criminal history check, but the law requires an individualized assessment about conviction history. This means that an employer cannot rescind the job offer without considering the nature and gravity of the criminal history, the time that has passed since the conviction, and the nature of the job being sought. If the employer decides to rescind the job offer based on criminal history, they must inform the applicant in writing, provide a copy of any conviction history report they relied on, and give at least five business days to respond.

In order to overcome these legal obligations, an employer must show that the conviction is job related and consistent with business necessity. In other words, it may be legitimate for a bank to refuse to hire a convicted bank robber. However, the bank would have difficulty showing that an employee convicted of jay-walking could not be a valued bank teller.

Negligent Hiring
Negligent hiring is a claim made by an injured party against an employer based on the theory that the employer knew or should have known about the employee's background which, if known, indicates a dangerous or untrustworthy character. E*van F. v. Hughson United Methodist Church*, (3d Dist. 1992) 8 Cal. App. 4th 828. It can also apply to negligent supervision and retention.

This can occur under any number of circumstances. For example, if a supervisor with a sexual assault conviction sexually assaults a subordinate, the employer can be sued for negligent hiring if the employer knew or should have known about the past conduct. Or if a delivery driver with a DUI conviction causes a fatal accident.

Wait. Doesn't Ban the Box prohibit those types of

questions?

Indeed, it does. Welcome to California, where employers can be held liable for both asking and not asking a question.

The best defense against a claim for negligent hiring is for an employer to prove that it exercised reasonable care. This is where record keeping becomes important. Detailed notes recording what was asked and answered in the employment application can be evidence that proper inquiries were made.

Also, remember that Ban the Box does not prohibit background checks. It merely controls the timing of when the background check can be performed. Employers should still take advantage of criminal background checks.

References

Here is some good news for employers. It is common practice for potential employers to call former employers for a reference on prospective employees. Traditionally, former employers were only permitted to provide basic information to prospective employers such as date of hire and whether the former employer would rehire the employee. Such communications are deemed to be privileged and protected from a lawsuit for defamation — if done without malice.

In 2019, California passed a law permitting former employers to disclose (a) complaints of sexual harassment by an employee to an employer based on credible evidence; (b) communications between the employer and interested persons regarding a complaint of sexual harassment; and (c) communications by the employer whether the employer's decision to not rehire the employee is based on the employer's determination that the former employee engaged in sexual harassment. Once again, this information must be conveyed without malice, which means the previous employer cannot call to "warn" the future employer.

Hiring employers should take advantage of this new law and ask former employers about sexual harassment claims. A sexual harassment lawsuit can be devastating and this is one avenue of information that California has made available to employers so that they can obtain information before hiring a potential harasser.

Drug Tests

Another available avenue for information is the drug test. For good reason, employers do not want to hire drug addicts. When an employee comes to work under the influence of a controlled substance, it increases the potential harm to customers, co-workers and/or company property. However, drug testing in the workplace should be done with caution because it is a violation of privacy. Many things can be learned from a blood or urine sample, including prescription drugs, a disability or even pregnancy.

There are varying rules when it comes to drug tests. The important thing to know is that hiring is the best time for drug testing. The courts have held that suspicionless drug testing is permissible as part of a "preplacement medical examination" applied to all new job applicants. However, it is impermissible to drug test current employees as a condition for a promotion. *Loder v. City of Glendale* (1997) 14 C4th 846, 898-899.

After being hired, employees have a greater right to privacy. Many employers mistakenly believe that random drug testing is permissible. However, the courts have held that it is only permissible when the employee is in "a safety or security sensitive position." *Smith v. Fresno Irrig. Dist.* (1999) 72 CA4th 147, 159.

The nature of the drug test, the equipment used, the manner of administration and its reliability are important factors in determining whether an employer can administer a drug test. "The primary focus of a state constitutional privacy claim in the employee drug testing context is a reasonable balancing test—balancing the drug test's intrusion on the reasonable expectations of the employee against the drug test's promotion of the employer's legitimate interests." *Kraslawsky v. Upper Deck Co.* (1997) 56 Cal.App.4th 179, 186-187.

Even if the invasion of privacy is justified, the employee may prevail on an action "by showing there are feasible and effective alternatives to defendant's conduct which have a lesser impact on privacy interests." *Hill v. National Collegiate Athletic Ass'n,* (2009) 7 Cal.4th 40. Therefore, it is best to consult an attorney before administering a drug test post-hiring.

It's All About Information

Hiring an employee is a lot like trying to pick the right cantaloupe at the grocery store. It is difficult to know whether the inside is good just by looking at the outside. Sure, everyone has a theory about how to pick the right melon, but nothing is certain. It is the same with hiring an employee. An applicant can have a sparkling resume and still turn out to be incompetent.

Information is the key. However, the state of California requires that information be obtained through non-discriminatory and non-invasive means.

CHAPTER FOUR
INDEPENDENT CONTRACTORS

Taxes. Taxes. Taxes.

The three least favorite words of any business. In California, employers are responsible for paying a portion of payroll taxes on behalf of their employees such as Unemployment Insurance Tax, Employment Training Tax, Social Security Tax, and Medicare Tax. On top of taxes, employers are required to carry workers compensation insurance and, possibly, provide other health insurance benefits to their employees.

But what if these expenses can be avoided by calling workers "independent contractors" rather than employees?

That is the ill-advised thinking of many liability-prone employers.

In recent years, the willful misclassification of employees as independent contractors has come under scrutiny by the state of California. The motivation?

Taxes.

In April 2018, the California Supreme Court, citing the theft of "billions of dollars in tax revenue," ruled on "what standard applies, under California law, in determining whether workers should be classified as employees or as independent contractors." *Dynamex Operations W. v. Superior Court*, (2018) 4 Cal. 5th 903, 914.

In this landmark ruling, the California Supreme Court definitively ruled that California courts would universally apply the "ABC Test."

"The ABC test **presumptively considers all workers to be employees**, and permits workers to be classified as independent contractors only if the hiring business demonstrates that the worker in question satisfies **each of three conditions**: (a) that the worker is free from the control and direction of the hirer in connection with the performance of the work, both under the contract for the performance of the work and in fact; and (b) that the worker performs work that is outside the usual course of the hiring entity's business; and (c) that the worker is customarily engaged in an independently established trade, occupation, or business of the same nature as that involved in the work performed. *Dynamex, supra*, 4 Cal. 5th 903 at 956, emphasis added.

On September 18, 2019, Governor Gavin Newsom signed into law, Assembly Bill 5 ("AB5"), codifying *Dynamex's* ABC Test. Upon signing AB5, Governor Newsom wrote, "The hallowing out of our middle-class has been 40 years in the making, and the need to create lasting economic security for our workforce demands action. Assembly Bill 5 is an important step. A next step is creating pathways for more workers to form a union, collectively bargain to earn more, and have a stronger voice at work – all while preserving flexibility and innovation."

AB5 states that it "shall apply retroactively to existing claims and actions to the maximum extent permitted by law." This means that there will be no forgiveness for employers who relied on the old standard when classifying independent contractors.

Since the ABC Test is now law, an examination of the three prongs is necessary.

1. "Free from the control and direction of the hiring entity"

"Control" has always been a key factor in determining employment classification. "The existence of the right of control and supervision establishes the existence of an agency relationship." *Malloy v. Fong* (1951) 37 Cal.2d 356, 370. There are many factors to consider in this prong of the analysis including supervision, scheduling, control of duties, and whether the employer provides training to the worker. As one Court stated, "Perhaps the strongest evidence of the right to control is whether the hirer can discharge the worker without cause, because '[t]he power of the principal to terminate the services of the agent gives him the means of controlling the agent's activities.'" *Ayala v. Antelope Valley Newspapers, Inc.* (2014) 59 Cal.4th 522, 532.

2. "Performs work that is outside the usual course of the hiring entity's business"

Under the second prong, employers are urged to adopt an outside perspective. The question to ask is, "Would the services be viewed by others as falling within the hiring entity's business rather than a worker's own independent business render that worker an employee and not a contractor?" For example, a retail store would not normally retain a plumber or electrician to perform maintenance work at the facility.

The label put on the relationship by the hiring business is not controlling and inquiry instead focuses on whether "the work done, in essence, follows the usual path of an employee." Employers must also understand the operations of a competing business. If competing businesses hire employees to perform comparable duties, then a court would be less likely to view the worker's independent contractor status as legitimate.

3. "Independently established trade, occupation, or business"

Under the third prong, businesses are required to prove that the worker is customarily engaged in an independently established trade, occupation, or business of the same nature as the work they are performing for the hiring entity. This will be the most difficult prong for employers to overcome. A business cannot unilaterally determine a worker's status simply by labeling the worker as an "independent contractor." Likewise, the employer cannot require the worker to enter into a contract that designates the worker an independent contractor as a condition of hiring. The Supreme Court held that term "independent contractor," refers to an individual who independently has made the decision to go into business for himself or herself. Such an individual generally takes the usual steps to establish and promote his or her independent business through incorporation, licensure, advertisements, routine offerings to provide the services of the independent business to the public or to a number of potential customers, and the like.

Exemptions

AB5 includes a number of occupations that would be exempt and, therefore, permitted to label certain workers as independent contractors. These exempt occupations would include, among others, licensed insurance agents, certain licensed health care professionals, registered securities broker-dealers or investment advisers, direct sales salespersons, real estate licensees, commercial fishermen, workers providing licensed barber or cosmetology services, and others performing work under a contract for professional services, with another business entity, or pursuant to a subcontract in the construction industry.

Unless covered by one of these exemptions, workers should never be classified as independent contractors. There is no clever way to avoid payroll taxes. This is the price of doing business in California.

The penalties for willfully misclassifying employees as independent contractors are severe. Under Labor Code § 228.6, the Labor and Workforce Development Agency can assess a civil penalty of between $5,000 and $25,000 per violation. As previously stated, this penalty is against any person and not just the corporation.

In addition, the employer will be liable for any additional wage and hour violations that arise from the misclassification such as overtime and missed meal period premiums.

Even if a business can meet all three-prongs of the ABC Test (control, work outside the course of business and independently established trade), an attorney should be retained to draft an up-to-date independent contractor agreement. Be cautious of free agreements online, which are neither current nor reflect California law.

CHAPTER FIVE
WAGES

Millions of years ago, some clever caveman realized that he had something of value... a cave. He offered the use of that cave to a wandering Neanderthal in exchange for hunting and gathering skills. This was the world's first employment relationship.

Probably.

The employment relationship predates written history, so we do not really know how it began. The point is that employment is a mutually beneficial union that is born from ingenuity. A skilled person makes tools. A savvy person pays others to make tools and sells them for a profit. It can well be said that the definition of a genius is someone who pays another to make money for them.

The problem was that some people turned savvy into selfish. Horrific employers reasoned that, if the workers were shackled, payment was unnecessary. Other discovered that entire generations of workers could be bound by the threat of being removed from land owned by feudal lords. In the case of indentured servitude, contractual agreements became the binding force.

Labor laws are a resulting consequence of scheming employers. For every employer that found clever and sometimes nefarious ways to save money at the expense of workers, a new law was created. This chapter reviews some of the most common California wage and hour laws that every employer should know.

Minimum Wage

California likes to believe it is at the forefront of labor laws. However, that is not always the case. For example, the ABC Test discussed in the previous chapter derived from Massachusetts law, which also happens to be the first state to implement a minimum wage in 1912. California followed four years later, and the Federal Labor Standards Act was signed by Franklin Delano Roosevelt in 1938. For trivia purposes, the world's first minimum wage law was passed in New Zealand in 1894.

Regardless of origin, California has ensured that it is at the forefront of minimum wage. In 2016, in response to the social movement "Fight for Fifteen," California passed a law that would gradually raise minimum wage to $15 per hour beginning on January 1, 2022. Since that time, California has maintained the highest minimum wage in the country, excluding Washington D.C. and a few select cities.

California employers need to be aware of their geographical locations because some cities, such as San Francisco and Los Angeles, have laws requiring a higher minimum wage. In fact, there are currently twenty-seven different minimum wage rates in California, which vary depending on geography, industry and number of employees. These rates can increase January 1 or July 1 of each year, so it is critical that employers stay apprised of minimum wage rate changes.

Due to constant change and variation, the current minimum wage cannot be identified in this book. The Department of Industrial Resource is the best place to find updated information on minimum wage laws.

Overtime

Labor Code § 510 establishes that all work performed in excess of eight hours per day or 40-hours per week "shall be compensated at the rate of no less than one and one-half times the regular rate of pay for an employee." Employees earn double the "regular rate" for work in excess of 12 hours per day.

Note that overtime must be paid after eight hours per day <u>or</u> 40 hours per week. The Federal Labor Standards Act (FLSA) only requires overtime after 40 hours in a workweek. There is no eight-hour per day requirement under federal law. Only California, Alaska and Nevada require overtime after eight hours of work. Colorado requires overtime after 12 hours.

One common pitfall for employers is the calculation of an employee's "regular rate." Although California law provides little guidance, the Department of Labor Standards Enforcement (DLSE) has stated that "(t)he regular rate of pay includes many different types of remuneration, for example: hourly earnings, salary, piecework earnings, commission, bonus, value of meals and lodging." [DLSE 2002 Enforcement Policies & Interpretations Manual (Revised), §§ 49.1-49.1.2.2]

Many employers calculate the hourly rate and then add commissions or bonuses. This is incorrect. The bonuses should be counted before calculating the time-and-a-half rate. In industries where the commissions cannot be calculated immediately, the employer is still obligated to apportion back to the hours worked when the commission was earned. [29 CFR § 778.119]

Another common source of liability is the calculation of "hours worked." California law defines "hours worked" as "the time during which an employee is subject to the control of an employer and includes all the time the employee is suffered or permitted to work, whether or not required to do so." The DLSE has interpreted this definition to extend beyond an employee's scheduled shift, including instances involving pre- and post-shift duties.

In the case of, *Ghazaryan v. Diva Limousine, Ltd.*, (2008) 169 Cal. App. 4th 1524, 1528, limousine drivers filed a class-action lawsuit for the time they were required to wait between pick-ups. Even though they were not performing any driving duties, they were still "suffered to work" while they waited for their next call.

Employers should not treat an employee willing to work off the clock as an asset. This is clear liability. Employees are willing to put in extra time when it may help to secure their job or gain favoritism. However, wage and hour claims typically come after separation of employment. When the employee moves on to the next job, he or she may come back looking for that unpaid overtime compensation. When (not if) that happens, there are severe civil penalties. Therefore, overtime should be closely monitored.

Exemptions

There are a number of exemptions from overtime and minimum wages. The three most common are 1) executive employees, 2) administrative employees, 3) professional employees. These exemptions depend on the primary duties performed by the employee and amount of compensation earned.

"Executive employees" are involved in the management of two or more employees and have authority to hire and fire. These employees must also customarily and regularly exercise discretionary judgment.

"Administrative employees" are those whose primary duties are directly related to management policies or general business operations of the employer or its customers, as distinguished from "production employees" whose primary duty is producing the goods or services that the employer produces. *Bell v. Farmers Ins. Exch.* (2001) 87 Cal.App.4th 805, 820.

"Professional employees" must be either licensed and "primarily engaged" in an enumerated profession, or "primarily engaged in an occupation commonly recognized as a learned or artistic profession." 8 CCR § 11010 *et seq*. These are jobs that require an advanced degree such as doctors, teachers and lawyers.

To qualify for one of these exemptions, the employee must earn a monthly salary equivalent to at least twice the state minimum wage for full-time employment. This is known as the "salary test."

If minimum wage is $12 per hour (remember, this varies by geographic location, industry and business size), a salaried employee must make $49,920 per year ($12 x 2 x 40 hours x 52 weeks = $49,920). When minimum wage reaches $15 per hour in 2022, salaried employees must be making at least $62,400 per year ($15 x 2 x 40 hours x 52 = $62,400).

Another common exemption is the outside salesperson. An "outside salesperson" is someone who regularly works more than half of his or her working time in sales activities outside the workplace. 8 CCR § 11010 *et seq*. If an employee spends a significant amount of time performing duties other than sales, or a substantial amount of time doing sales calls while inside the employer's office building, then that employee's job may not qualify for the outside salesperson exemption.

There may be other exemptions depending on the industry.

Alternative Workweeks

California's adherence to the eight-hour workday causes a unique problem that does not occur in a majority of states. For example, imagine a common situation where both parents in a two-income household work full-time. Child care is expensive and the parents would prefer that at least one of them be home with the children as often as possible. With both parents working five 8-hour shifts, daycare is required at least three days per week. However, the clever parents realize that if they both worked four 10-hour shifts, they would only need daycare one day per week.

Simple solution, right? Not in California.

In California, alternative workweek schedules are only permissible when an employer adheres to an election process set forth in Labor Code § 511. Individual employees are not granted the authority to negotiate an alternative workweek by agreeing to waive overtime.

In order for an employer to implement an alternative workweek schedule, they must:
1. Provide written notice of their intent to adopt an alternative workweek schedule;
2. The employer must then host a meeting regarding the effects of the alternative workweek on the employees' wages, hours and benefits.
3. 14 days after the meeting, alternative schedule must be approved by a two-thirds vote of the affected employees in the work unit. A "work unit" is defined in the California wage orders to include all employees in a readily identifiable work unit, such as a division, a department, a job classification, a shift, a separate physical location, or a recognized subdivision of any such work unit. A work unit may consist of one employee as long as the requirements for an identifiable work unit are met.
4. The vote must be conducted by secret ballot

at the workplace.
5. The employer must also provide a "menu" of options with alternative workweek options. Employees are free to choose their schedule from this menu.

If the alternative workweek schedule is approved, the employer must notify the DLSE and be placed in a database. Due to this overly complicated process, most employers do not attempt to implement alternative workweek schedules. If administered incorrectly, the employer would be liable for all the unpaid overtime incurred during that period of time.

As a result, the 8-hour workday has become the standard of California employment. While operating a jackhammer for an extra two hours per day might not be enticing, a 10-hour shift could have appeal in less-strenuous administrative positions. Unfortunately, California has removed all individualism when it comes to wage and hour laws.

Timely Payment of Wages

"California has long regarded the timely payment of employee wage claims as indispensable to the public welfare." For this reason, courts have held that it is "essential to the public welfare" that employees receive their pay when it is due, and that an "employer who knows that wages are due, has ability to pay them, and still refuses to pay them, acts against good morals and fair dealing, and necessarily intentionally does an act which prejudices the rights of his employee.'" *Smith v. Superior Court* (2006) 39 Cal.4th 77, 82 (quoting *In re Trombley* (1948) 31 Cal.2d 801, 809-810).

Every employer must "keep posted conspicuously at the place of work, if practicable, or otherwise where it can be seen as employees come and go to their places of work, or at the office or nearest agency for payment kept by the employer, a notice specifying the regular pay days and the time and place of payment ..." Labor Code § 207.

Non-exempt employees must be paid twice each calendar month. Wages earned between the 1st and 15th of the month must be paid between the 16th and 26th. Wages earned between the 16th and the end of the month must be paid between the 1st and 10th of the following month. Labor Code § 204.

Labor Code § 201(a) provides that, if an employer discharges an employee, wages earned and unpaid at the time of the discharge are due and payable immediately. (For employees who separate employment voluntarily, Labor Code § 202(a) requires the payment of wages within 72 hours, unless the employee has given 72 hours previous notice of his or her intention to quit, in which case the employee is entitled to his or her wages at the time of quitting.)

If an employer willfully fails to pay wages due to an employee who is discharged or quits, the law sets forth a penalty equal to the employee's daily wages for each day, not exceeding 30 days, that the wages are unpaid. This is in addition to the unpaid wages. *Amaral v. Cintas* (2008) 163 Cal.App.4th 1157, 1201.

The best way to avoid liability is to pay employees on time.

Wage Statements

California Labor Code § 226(a) requires an employer to furnish its employees with an accurate itemized statement in writing showing, among other things: (a) gross wages earned; (b) net wages earned; (c) total hours worked by the employee, *except* for any employee whose compensation is *solely based on a salary and who is* exempt from payment of overtime under subdivision (a) of Section 515 or any applicable order of the Industrial Welfare Commission; (d) all applicable hourly rates in effect during the pay period and the corresponding number of hours worked at each hourly rate by the employee.

An employee suffering injury as a result of a knowing and intentional failure by an employer to comply with subdivision (a) is entitled to recover the greater of all actual damages or fifty dollars ($50) for the initial pay period in which violation occurs and one hundred dollars ($100) per employee for each violation in a subsequent pay period, not to exceed an aggregate penalty of four thousand dollars ($4,000), and is entitled to an award of costs and reasonable attorney's fees. Labor Code § 226 (e)(1).

Third-party payroll companies are useful in providing wage statements, but they tend to stay away from giving legal advice regarding wage statement compliance. Even if using one of these services, wage statements should be reviewed for correct information.

Failure to Reimburse in Violation of Labor Code § 2802

Employers are required to reimburse employees for all expenditures or losses that: (1) were incurred in direct consequence of the employee's discharge of his or her duties, or obedience to the directions of the employer; and (2) were necessary. (Cal. Lab. Code § § 2800, 2802; see also *Nicholas Laboratories, LLC v. Chen* (2011) 199 Cal.App.4th 1240, 1249 citing *Cassady v. Morgan, Lewis & Bockius* (2006) *LLP* 145 Cal.App.4th 220, 230.)

To show liability for an employer's failure to reimburse an employee for necessary expenditures, an employee need only show that he or she was required to use personal items for work-related purposes, and he or she was not reimbursed. *Cochran v. Schwan's Home Service, Inc.*, (2014) 228 Cal. App. 4th 1137.

This is most common with vehicle mileage. If an employer requires that an employee uses his or her personal vehicle to run an errand for the employer, mileage must be paid to compensate the employee for use of the vehicle. Other examples of possible reimbursements could include cellphone or laptop use.

Stay in the Box

Entrepreneurs are blessed with the ability to "think outside the box." While that is good in the context or marketing, it is not good when it comes to wages. The state of California wants employers to stay in the box so that they be managed. In fact, the Department of Industrial Relations has issue 17 wage orders setting forth specific wages laws according to industry. Every business in California falls under one of these industries and must abide by the designated wage order.

It is important to know which wage order is applicable because they have different rules regarding payment of wages. For example, the agricultural industry is permitted to work employees 60 hours per week before paying overtime. However, a grocery store cannot claim to be in the agricultural industry just because it sells produce. That is the type of outside the box thinking that will create a class action lawsuit.

CHAPTER SIX
MEAL AND REST PERIODS

By now, it is probably obvious that California creates employment laws the same way a gambler would play with house money. Federal law requires overtime after 40 hours per week; California raises the bet to require overtime after eight hours per day. Federal minimum wage is $7.25 per hour; California doubles down with $15 per hour.

Why not? Stricter labor laws do no decrease California's tax revenue. (In the case of minimum wage, tax revenue will actually increase.) Businesses are left holding the debt.

Rest periods follow the same pattern. Federal law does not currently require employers to provide meal or rest periods for their employees. However, it does permit states to make meal and rest period requirements. Currently, twenty-one states have meal period requirements. Only seven states (California, Colorado, Kentucky, Minnesota, Nevada, Oregon, and Washington) have meal <u>and</u> rest period requirements.

Meal Periods

Under California law, employers must provide employees with no less than a thirty-minute meal period for shifts exceeding more than five hours. A second meal period is required if an employee works more than ten hours per day. Labor Code § 512. An employer is not required to police meal periods. However, an employer must do more than simply make meal periods available. The employer must relieve the employees of all duty, relinquish control over their activities and must not impede or discourage employees from taking a meal period.

There are only two circumstances where a meal period can be waived. The first occurs when the total work period of the employee is no more than six hours and the meal period is waived by mutual consent of both the employer and employee. The second occurs between the tenth and twelfth hours of work. Recall that after ten hours, an employee is entitle to two meal periods. If the first meal period was not waived, the employee can waive the second meal period by mutual consent.

Here is a useful summary:

Between 0 and 5 Hours – No meal period required
Between 5.1 and 6 Hours – One meal period that may be waived by mutual consent
Between 6.1 and 10 Hours – One mandatory meal period, which cannot be waived
Between 10.1 and 12 Hours – Two meal periods, only the second may be waived by mutual consent
Over 12 Hours – Two mandatory meal periods

"As a statutorily protected right, the decision to

forego a meal period must be made personally by each worker on a daily basis. The decision to forego a meal period may not, therefore, be based on a specific requirement of the employer or on a policy or practice which could reasonably be perceived to be a condition of employment. Therefore, blanket 'waivers' of meal periods or 'group' agreements to forego or forestall meal periods until later in the work day, whether written or oral, will not be considered valid." V*alenzuela v. Giumarra Vineyards Corp.*, 614 F. Supp. 2d 1089, 1095 (E.D. Cal. 2009).

Under some circumstances, a meal period may be taken "on duty." An on-duty meal period is permitted only when 1) the nature of the work prevents an employee from being relieved of all duty, 2) there is a written agreement between the employer and employee and 3) the agreement states that the employee may revoke the agreement at any time. IWC Orders 1-15, Section 11, Order 16, Section 10. If the employer requires the employee to remain at the work site or facility during the meal period, the meal period must be paid. This is true even where the employee is relieved of all work duties during the meal period. *Bono Enterprises, In. v. Bradshaw* (1995) 32 Cal.App.4th 968.

Rest Periods

In general, employees must be provided paid duty-free rest periods of 10 minutes of rest for every 4 hours worked. For shifts of less than 4 hours, employees are entitled to a 10-minute rest period after 3 1/2 hours.

These rest periods must be in the middle of the

shift "insofar as practicable." In other words, the employer cannot make the employee take the rest periods at the beginning of the shift. Likewise, employees cannot take rest periods at the end of a shift to leave early.

The issue of whether employers must ensure that breaks are taken or only simply provide breaks has been a source of significant litigation. In the land mark case of *Brinker Restaurant Corp. v. Superior Court,* the California Supreme Court ultimately ruled that employers do not have to ensure employees take their meal breaks, only provide them. Once the meal period is provided, there is no duty to police meal breaks to ensure that no work is being done. *See Brinker Restaurant Corp. v. Superior Court* (2012) 53 Cal.4th 1004.

Rest periods are separate from restroom breaks and, in fact, the Industrial Welfare Commission requires suitable resting facilities be in an area "separate from toilet rooms."

Exemptions

Meal and rest periods are only mandatory for nonexempt employees, which means the same exemptions discussed in the previous chapter apply (i.e. Executive, Administrative, Professional and Outside sales).

While the exemption is certainly beneficial to employers, it has always seemed rather out of place. After all, California is a state that proudly promotes workplace equality. Yet, an employee's pay scale determines their entitlement to lunch breaks. If an employee is more educated and highly paid, the government does not feel a need to dictate when and how breaks are administered.

Lactation Breaks

California law requires that all employers to provide all lactating employees with a "reasonable amount of time" throughout the day to express breast milk. In addition, the employer must provide a private room or space, other than a toilet stall, in which to express breast milk.

The only exception is if providing lactation breaks or a private space to express breast milk would "seriously disrupt" the operations of the employer. For this exception to apply, there must be a significant burden on the employer; minor inconvenience will not qualify.

The Consequences

If an employee is forced to miss a meal or rest period, he or she must be paid one hour of pay at the regular rate of compensation for each workday that the meal period is not provided. This is referred to as "premium pay." If the employer fails to pay the premium pay, the employee can file a wage claim with the Division of Labor Standards Enforcement or bring in action in state or federal court.

An employer who violates the California lactation accommodation law may be penalized $100 per violation by the state labor commissioner.

CHAPTER SEVEN
EMPLOYEE HANDBOOKS

The importance of an employee handbook cannot be understated. As long as the handbook is drafted properly, and the policies are followed, an employee handbook can be used as both a sword and shield to protect the employer from liability.

As a shield, an employee handbook helps reduce potential liability. One of the greatest benefits of having an employee handbook is its potential to protect companies from employees' legal claims. An employee handbook can be used to assist the employer in avoiding and defending against discrimination, harassment and wrongful discharge claims.

As a sword, the employee handbook allows employers to be proactive. An employee handbook should articulate the employer's expectations by clearly describing the employer's policies and procedures. This includes the actions supervisors and employees should take when an employee has a problem or grievance. Employers should not wait until a lawsuit is filed before learning about what occurs in the workplace. In addition, one of the goals of an employee handbook should be to promote fairness and evenhanded treatment of employees by establishing uniform standards that can be applied by all employees.

For example, if the employee handbook clearly establishes a policy against harassment, it conveys that the employer is serious about protecting its employees. However, the protection only exists as long as the policy is being enforced. The employee handbook should also establish policies and procedures for handling harassment claims, including reserving the right to terminate the harasser. Thus, without a proactive sword, the employer may lose its shield.

Many employers believe that employee handbooks hinder flexibility. While this may be true of a poorly drafted handbook, a properly drafted handbook will actually incorporate a necessary degree of flexibility. However, the advantages of an employee handbook greatly outweigh their potential drawbacks.

Employee handbooks should be straight-forward and drafted in simple language. Legal jargon should be avoided. Never include policies and procedures to which the company does not adhere. An employee handbook creates a contract between employers and employees. It should be regularly updated to reflect changes in the law. When in doubt, seek guidance from a qualified employment lawyer.

Employee handbook resources are readily available online. However, it is always a good idea to consult an attorney for update-to-date laws. Standard policies available online may not be applicable to your business. In addition, there are many small but important policies that are omitted from "one size fits all" handbooks. Here are a few essential policies that all handbooks should include:

1. Policy Against Unlawful Harassment
2. Equal Opportunity Statements
3. Commitment to Interactive Process under Disability Discrimination
4. Right to Revise
5. Medical Leaves of Absence
6. Employee Classifications
7. Employment-at-will Statements
8. Disciplinary Policies
9. Payroll and Salary Practice Policies
10. Family and Medical Leave Policies
11. Pregnancy Leave Policies
12. Health and Safety Policies
13. Workplace Security and Violence Prevention Policies
14. Reference Requests
15. Dispute Resolution Procedures
16. Privacy Policies
17. Benefit Description Disclaimer
18. Internet, E-mail, Social Media and Electronic Communication Policy
19. Exit Interview Policies
20. Acknowledgement Form

Remember, employee handbooks are living documents that must evolve with the law. As fast as laws change in California, it can well be said that every handbook needs revision.

CHAPTER EIGHT
RECORD-KEEPING REQUIREMENTS

When Thomas Jefferson commissioned an expedition to explore the western frontier in 1803, he called upon two men who, among other things, were valiant record-keepers. Meriwether Lewis, a secretary, and William Clark, a cartographer, spent three years exploring and documenting an unknown territory. Some of the most important things to come from the Lewis and Clark Expedition were their personal journals, which contained invaluable information used by those who followed their trail westward.

The value of record-keeping cannot be overstated. Advanced civilizations require written language, arts, sciences and government – which all begin with record-keeping. The same can be said about business. While all businesses keep records, there is a significant difference between a cave painting and the Great Library of Alexandria. Unfortunately, some business owners remain in the stone age of record-keeping, which can create significant liability.

Both Federal and State law require employers to create and maintain employment records. This includes payroll records, employee's name, address, occupation, hours worked each day and week, wages paid and date of payment, amounts earned as straight-time pay and overtime, and deductions. These records must be maintained for three years. Labor Code §§ 226(a), 1174(d), 29 CFR § 516.5. Other records, such as time and earning cards and work schedules must be kept for two years. 29 CFR § 516.6.

As previously discussed, California law requires employers to provide employees with wage statements (also known as pay stubs). The wage statement requirement provides employees with an opportunity to calculate the wages owed to them. To illustrate the need for accurate wage statements, imagine playing blackjack at a casino and having a hand totaling twenty. There would be outrage at the table if the dealer claims to have cards totaling twenty-one without showing the full hand. Just as gaming rules require blackjack dealers to show all their cards, the law requires that employers provide a full accounting of employee wages.

Current and former employees (or a representative) also have the right to inspect and receive a copy of their personnel files and records that relate to the employee's performance or to any grievance concerning the employee. Labor Code § 1198.5. A violation of this provision is a penalty of $750 and attorneys' fees should the employee be required to sue for the records. Under Labor Code §

1174.5, an employer who willfully fails to maintain records is subject to a civil penalty of $500.

If the civil penalties are not enough to discourage poor record-keeping, consider the ramifications it can have during litigation. If an employee alleges unpaid overtime, the employer will not be able to receive the benefit of poor record-keeping. If time sheets and payroll records are absent, a jury may consider the employee's reasonable calculation of damages. In this situation, an employer can be found liable for an amount greater than the actual offense.

The best advice for an employer is to maintain accurate records and "show its hand" when required to do so. Being able to show favorable cards can prevent or win a lawsuit, so employers should strive to have records that accurately show compliance with the law. A good business is built upon a foundation of accurate record-keeping.

CHAPTER NINE
LEAVES OF ABSENCE

A corporation exists to make money. It's that simple. A human, on the other hand, exists to... well, that is life's ultimate question.

While the law treats corporations like living beings, they are not *human* beings. A corporation does not suffer from the frailties of mortality. A corporation does not become ill. A corporation does not ache at the loss of a loved one. A corporation does not need time off. It can operate perpetually - as long as there are humans to operate it.

This co-dependent relationship becomes strained when there is an extended leave of absence. The reality of human frailty means that, at some point, every person requires extended time off to deal with a personal or medical issue. If the leave of absence is too long, the corporation begins to suffer financially. When the corporation loses profits, the employee's job is at risk.

In the 1980s the federal government debated the issue of how much job protection a worker should receive when there is a medical necessity. This was an especially important issue with women who wished to work and raise a family. The Pregnancy Discrimination Act was passed in 1978, but it did not address the return to work after pregnancy.

In 1984, Congress drafted the Family Employment Security Act (FESA), which called for up to twenty-six weeks (six months) per year of unpaid, job-protected leave to care for a new child, a child's illness, a spouse's disability, or the employee's own disability. That timeframe was rejected by pro-business legislators.

From 1986 to 1990, legislators debated the requirements of medical leave. President George H. W. Bush vetoed two other versions of the bill, stating that he supported family leave, but only if businesses were allowed to provide it voluntarily.

Finally, in 1993, the Family Medical Leave Act ("FMLA") was signed into law by newly elected President Bill Clinton with 73% approval from the United States Senate. The bill stated that "it is important for the development of children and the family unit that fathers and mothers be able to participate in early childrearing… [and] the lack of employment policies to accommodate working parents can force individuals to choose between job security and parenting."

What was the number decided by this decades-long debate? 12 weeks.

FMLA/CFRA

Under the FMLA and the California equivalent, the California Family Rights Act ("CFRA"), authorizes eligible employees to take up to a total of 12 weeks of paid or unpaid job-protected leave during a 12-month period. Eligible employees can take the leave for the birth of a child or adoption or foster care placement of a child, to care for an immediate family member (spouse, child or parent) with a serious health condition, or when the employee is unable to work because of a serious health condition.

Private employers are covered by the FMLA/CFRA if they have employed 50 or more employees for each working day during each of 20 or more calendar workweeks in the current or preceding calendar year. This was intended to protect small businesses from the impact of extended leaves of absence.

To be eligible for leave under the FMLA or CFRA, an employee must be 1) employed by the employer for at least 12 months as of the date leave commences; 2) employed for at least 1,250 hours of service during the 12-month period immediately preceding commencement of the leave; and 3) employed at a worksite where the employer employs at least 50 employees within 75 miles.

Both the FMLA and CFRA provide a right to leaves of absence for a maximum of 12 weeks unpaid leave in a 12-month period. The employer is permitted to decide how to calculate the leave year (i.e. calendar year, hire date, or rolling period). If an employer fails to select a calculation method, the choice providing "the most beneficial outcome for the employee" will be used.

While on leave, employees keep the same

employer-paid health benefits they had while working.

Pregnancy Leave

In addition to FMLA/CFRA, pregnant women are protected by the California Pregnancy Disability Leave Law (PDLL). PDLL requires employers to provide employees up to four months of leave for disability due to an employee's pregnancy, childbirth or related medical conditions. All employees of covered employers under the FEHA are eligible for leave, transfers and reasonable accommodation under the PDLL.

Maternity leave laws can be complicated, so here is a summary of key things to know:

PDLL runs concurrently with leave taken under the FMLA but not with CFRA. Rather, CFRA leave and pregnancy disability leave are two separate and distinct rights that employees have under California law. What this means is that the 12 weeks of CFRA leave can be taken after the four months of PDLL. If the maximum amount of both types of leave is taken, the total leave entitlement will be four months plus 12 workweeks (four months of pregnancy disability leave under the PDLL, of which 12 weeks may also be FMLA leave plus 12 workweeks of CFRA leave).

However, it should be noted that an employee is only entitled to use the maximum amount of pregnancy disability leave if she was actually disabled by pregnancy for four months, and is entitled to the CFRA leave only if she meets CFRA eligibility rules and has not previously used the CFRA leave for another purpose. In other words, a leave of absence of morning sickness may reduce the post-delivery leave.

Bonding Leave

A leave of absence for the birth of a child is not exclusive to new mothers. The law provides new parents to take "bonding leave" as governed by certain statutory requirements.

As previously stated, FMLA and CFRA provide job security to an employee who is absent from work because of the employee's own serious health condition or to care for specified family members with serious health conditions, as well as for the birth of a child and to care for a newborn child, or because of the placement for adoption or foster care of a child with the employee. Under FMLA and CFRA, both the mother and father are entitled to leave to bond with the newborn even if the newborn does not have a serious health condition. See 29 CFR § 825.120(a)(2).

The New Parent Leave Act (NPLA), which became effective on January 1, 2018, applies to smaller employers with 20-49 employees. (FMLA and CFRA cover 50 or more employees). Gov. Code § 12945.6. The NPLA requires employers with at least 20 employees to provide up to 12 workweeks of parental leave for eligible employees to bond with a new child within one year of the child's birth, adoption or foster care placement.

The qualifications for leave under FMLA, CFRA, and NPLA are generally the same. Employees are eligible to take child care or bonding leave if they have worked for an employer for 12 months, have at least 1,250 hours of service with the employer in the prior 12-month period, and who work at a worksite in which the employer employs at the qualified number of employees within 75 miles of the employee.

The NPLA does not provide extra leave for employees already eligible to take baby-bonding leave under the CFRA or the FMLA. Employees already eligible to take parental bonding leave under the CFRA and/or the FMLA are not eligible to take NPLA leave. Gov. Code § 12945.6(c). Employees may take California Pregnancy Disability leave in addition to NPLA leave, if the employee is otherwise qualified for that leave. Gov. Code § 12945.6(b).

Leave under FMLA, CFRA, and NPLA is unpaid unless available paid time off is taken (e.g., vacation, paid sick time or paid personal time off) and/or unless disability or other income replacement benefits are available (e.g., California State Disability Insurance, California Paid Family Leave, workers' compensation payments, and/or payments from an employer's short-term or long-term disability pay plan).

Since bonding time does not require a medical condition, it can be taken at any time but must be concluded within one year of the birth. 29 CFR § 825.120(a)(2). Both men and women are eligible for leave for the birth and to care for a newborn. 29 CFR § 825.120(a)(1). Leave taken before the birth of a child is FMLA leave for the mother's serious health condition, not leave for the birth of a child. 29 CFR § 825.120(a)(4).

It is important to note that there is a time limit on

the bonding leave – one year after the birth or adoption. Therefore, if the employee has a child after six months of service, the window for bonding leave would be six months after leave qualification. This is the only type of leave that has such a limitation. Another limitation is that employers may limit leave rights if a husband and wife are employed by the same employer. Under these circumstances, the husband and wife are allotted a combined 12 weeks.

Sick Leave

California has some of the most progressive sick time laws in the country. At a minimum, California law requires the employers provide 24 hours (or 3 days) of paid sick leave per year for full-time employees, which can be used beginning on the 90th day of employment. Labor Code § 246.

California's sick time laws are actually very complex, primarily because employers are able to choose from different methods of accrual.

The accrual method: In this default method, eligible employees will start to earn at least one hour of paid leave for every 30 hours worked as soon as they begin their employment. As an employer, you can limit the amount of paid sick leave that employees may use each year to 24 hours, or three days, and limit the total hours accrued each year to 48 hours, or six days. The year starts on the employee's hire date and any unused paid sick leave can be carried over into the next year.

The lump sum method: Employers can elect to offer employees a set amount of paid leave upfront. Under this option, employers must provide at least

24 hours, or 3 days, of paid leave at the beginning of each 12-month period. These hours can be specifically for sick leave, or they can be earmarked for different uses, as long as those uses include sick leave.

Under both methods, new hires still have to wait 90 days before they can use their sick leave.

Employers may also elect to have a paid time off (PTO) policy. PTO policies provide a bank of hours in which the employer pools sick days, vacation days, and personal days that allows employees to use as the need or desire arises.

Some employers forego all the math and provide an unlimited paid time off policy. Due to the potential for abuse, this is not recommended. After all, businesses need employees to make money.

Terminating an Employee After Leave

This is one of the most difficult situations to navigate. Let's say an employee suffers a back injury and requires a medical leave of absence. Under FMLA/CFRA, the employee is only allowed 12 weeks of job protection. The employee can be terminated after the 12 weeks, right?

Wrong.

The Americans with Disabilities Act ("ADA") and FEHA create additional obligations for an employer to "reasonably accommodate" the employee's disability. In some cases, granting an additional leave of absence can serve as the reasonable accommodation.

What makes this situation tricky is that the California legislature has never defined how much leave must be granted until the reasonable accommodation obligation is met. After all, an employer is not obligated to keep an employee's job open forever.

So, how much leave should be given? One Week? One Month? One Year? No one knows. That's the trap California has set. Everything is on a case-by-case basis. An employer is not required to make an accommodation if it would impose an "undue hardship" on the operation of the employer's business. "Undue hardship" is defined as an action requiring significant difficulty or expense when considering several factors, including the nature and cost of the accommodation in relation to the size, resources, nature, and structure of the employer's operation.

Since each situation must be evaluated on a case-by-case basis, the following are general guidelines to assist in protecting employers from potential litigation:

1. Carefully administer FMLA leave, keeping track of relevant dates. (There may be additional requirements for pregnancy and worker's compensation injuries).
2. Communicate regularly with the employee while he or she is on FMLA leave (and additional leave beyond FMLA, if granted).
3. Request documentation from the employee (or employee's doctor) stating when the employee may return to work.
4. Individually assess the employee's return to work and determine whether a reasonable accommodation is available.

5. If a reasonable accommodation is not available (including additional leave), be prepared to articulate how the continued absence significantly impacts business operations.

The important thing to remember is that the process requires "communication and good-faith exploration of possible accommodations between employers and individual employees with a known physical or mental disability with the goal of identifying an accommodation that allows the employee to perform the job effectively." *Jensen v. Wells Fargo Bank*, (2000) 85 Cal. App. 4th 245, 261.

CHAPTER TEN
WORKPLACE SAFETY

The Industrial Revolution, which culminated in the latter half of the 18th century, transformed largely rural societies into industrialized ones through new manufacturing processes. While manufacturing and job creation boomed, so too did workplace injuries.

However, without statutory rights, injured workers had to rely on common law negligence claims to recover damages for their injuries. Those who had the financial means to pursue an action in court were often defeated by the employer's defense that the employee assumed the risk or was injured through the negligence of a co-worker.

Massachusetts was the first state in the nation to pass safety and health legislation in 1877, establishing an affirmative duty for the employer to maintain safe machinery. By 1890, 21 states made statutory provisions for health hazards.

At the federal level, President William Howard Taft established the Department of Labor in 1913, which began to keep statistics on industrial accidents. The Bureau of Labor Standards was created by Labor Department President, Frances Perkins, in 1934.

By 1970, Congress was determined to pass legislation on workplace safety. At that time, approximately 14,000 occupational fatalities were being reported each year as well as 2.5 million job-related disabilities and 300,000 new cases of job-related illnesses. The Occupational Safety and Health Act was signed into law on December 29, 1970, by President Richard M. Nixon.

California followed the example of the federal government by passing the Occupational Safety and Health Act of 1973 ("Cal-OSHA") to enforce effective standards, assist and encourage employers to maintain safe and healthful working conditions, and to provide for enforcement, research, information, education and training in the field of occupational safety and health

California's Occupational Safety and Health Act of 1973 ("Cal-OSHA") requires that employers provide "safe and healthful working conditions for all California working men and women." Labor Code § 6300.

Cal-OSHA has jurisdiction over every "employment" and "place of employment" in California—i.e., any place where any trade, enterprise, business, or work is carried on involving any person engaged or permitted to work for hire. Labor Code §§ 6303(a), (b), 6307.

There are thousands of safety standards contained in Cal-OSHA. Many are applicable to only certain industries. However, there are some General Industry Safety Orders applicable to all California employers.

Employers must:
- Provide their employees with work and workplaces that are safe and healthful.
- Be aware of the hazards their employees face on the job, train every worker about the specific hazards on each job assignment, and keep records of this training.
- Correct any hazardous conditions that they know may result in serious injury to their employees. Failure to do so could result in criminal charges, monetary penalties, and even jail.
- Comply with all applicable Cal-OSHA standards, including training requirements.
- Notify the nearest Cal-OSHA office of any serious injury or fatality that occurs on the job, or any serious illness caused by the job. This must be done immediately after calling for emergency help to assist the injured worker.
- Display Cal-OSHA's Safety and Health Protection on the Job poster so that workers are aware of basic rights and responsibilities. This poster is also available in Spanish.

Injury and Illness Prevention Program

Employers in California are required to have an effective written Injury and Illness Prevention Program (IIPP). The IIPP should be custom tailored to each individual workplace. However, generally,

IIPP's should include the following elements:
1. Responsibility – The IIPP must identify who is responsible for the program.
2. Compliance – The IIPP must contain a system for ensuring that employees comply with safe and healthy work practices.
3. Communication – The IIPP must include a system to communicate with workers on health and safety matters, which must include a way for workers to report unsafe conditions without fear of reprisal.
4. Hazard Assessment – A system to identify unsafe or unhealthful conditions. This must include regular inspections of the worksite. Supervisors must be informed of any problems found.
5. Accident/Exposure Investigation – A system to investigate any job-related injuries and illnesses that occur.
6. Hazard Correction – A system to correct hazards in a timely manner.
7. Training and Instruction – Training for workers about the specific hazards on their jobs before they start work and every time a new hazard is introduced. Training must be in a form readily understandable by all workers.
8. Recordkeeping – Employers ordinarily must keep records of "scheduled and periodic inspections" and training for at least one year. However, employers with fewer than 10 employees may elect to maintain these records only until the hazard is corrected.

Ergonomics

In 1994, California declared war on Repetitive Motion Injuries (RMIs) by requiring businesses to adopt standards for ergonomics. Labor Code § 6357.

Every employer covered by the standard must implement a program to minimize RMIs. The program must include a worksite evaluation, correction of exposures that cause RMI (i.e. repetition) and employee training.

This is one of the few laws that provides employers with a "safe harbor" defense. An ergonomic program that adheres to these requirements will satisfy the employer's obligation under the ergonomics regulation unless it is shown that the employer knew of, but did not implement, a measure (a) substantially certain to cause a greater reduction in RMIs and (b) that would not have imposed additional unreasonable costs. 8 CCR § 5110(c).

Workplace Smoking

Under Labor Code § 6404.5, no employer shall "knowingly or intentionally" permit, and no person shall engage in, smoking tobacco products in an enclosed place at any place of employment. The ban on workplace smoking does not apply to certain places of employment, such as hotel/motel guestrooms, designated smoking areas, tobacco shops, private smokers' lounges, truck cabs (if nonsmoking employees are not present). A violation of this statute is an infraction and punishable by fine.

Heat Illness

"Heat illness" is a medical condition resulting from the body's inability to cope with a particular heat load, including heat stroke, cramps, exhaustion and syncope. 8 CCR § 3395(b). Businesses that are considered "outdoor places of employment" must provide shade and potable water to employees whenever the temperature in the work area reaches 80 degrees Fahrenheit. For certain industries (such as agricultural and construction), high-heat procedures must be implemented when the temperature equals or exceeds 95 degrees Fahrenheit.

Communicable Illnesses

In 2009, California sought to reduce the spread of airborne infectious diseases such as tuberculosis, meningococcal meningitis, measles, varicella, and influenza. 8 CCR § 5199. The standard applies to employers in the health care industry as well as certain other employers with elevated risk (e.g., correctional facilities, homeless shelters, drug treatment programs, laboratories capable of aerosolizing ATDs). The standard generally excludes dental offices and outpatient medical specialty practices that do not treat these diseases.

Hazardous Substances Disclosure

A hazardous material is any material, because of its quantity, concentration, physical or chemical characteristics, poses a significant present or potential hazard to human health and safety or the environment if released into the work place or the environment; or any material that is required to have a Material Safety Data Sheet according to Title 8, Section 339 of the California Code of Regulations.

Labels are required if the business handles or stores hazardous materials in quantities equal to or greater than threshold quantities of 55 gallons of a liquid, 500 pounds of a solid, and 200 cubic feet of a gas.

Proposition 65 (Safe Drinking Water and Toxic Enforcement Act, Health & Saf.C. § 25249.2 et seq.) requires certain business owners to provide a warning to persons who may be exposed at their place of business to "chemicals known to the state to cause cancer or reproductive toxicity."

Workplace Violence

Workplace violence is any act or threat of physical violence, harassment, intimidation, or other threatening disruptive behavior that occurs at the work site. It ranges from threats and verbal abuse to physical assaults and even homicide.

Unfortunately, workplace violence is becoming more prominent in the United States. According to Fed-OSHA, approximately two million people each year report some type of workplace violence. It is estimated that 25 percent of workplace violence goes unreported. The Bureau of Labor Statistics Census of Fatal Occupational Injuries (CFOI), reported that, of the 5,147 fatal workplace injuries that occurred in the United States in 2017, 458 were cases of intentional injury by another person.

In the case of *Franklin v. Monadock Co.* (2007) 151 Cal.App.4th 252, the court addressed workplace violence and held, "Labor Code section 6400 et seq.

and Code of Civil Procedure section 527.8, when read together, establish an explicit public policy requiring employers to provide a safe and secure workplace, including a requirement that an employer take reasonable steps to address credible threats of violence in the workplace."

Labor Code § 527.8, part of the Workplace Violence Safety Act, permits an employer to seek a temporary restraining order and an injunction on behalf of an employee against "a credible threat of violence from any individual, that can reasonably be construed to be carried out or to have been carried out at the workplace."

The *Franklin* court took the permissibility of a restraining and made it a duty under Cal-OSHA. The logic is simple. If a workplace has a loose electrical wire, the employer has a duty to fix it. If the employer knows about an individual with a "loose wire" and it poses a realistic threat to an employer, there is a similar duty to act.

"Credible threat of violence" means intentionally saying something or acting in a way that would make a reasonable person afraid for his or her safety or the safety of his or her family. An individual's history of threatening conduct may be considered in assessing whether particular conduct is threatening. *City of San Jose v. Garbett*, (6th Dist. 2010) 190 Cal. App. 4th 526.

CHAPTER ELEVEN
HARASSMENT

Harassment is a word that everyone knows but few understand. Employees like to throw around words like "harassment" and "hostile work environment" because these words tend to get an employer's attention – and rightly so. Defending a harassment lawsuit can be very costly.

However, employees and employers alike fail to completely understand what constitutes a "hostile work environment." Let's start with an example:

Adam likes hats and wears one to work every day. Carl thinks Adam's hat is ugly and makes it known to everyone. Adam feels he is being harassed by Carl because of the repeated criticism of his hat.

This might seem like a juvenile example, but petty squabbles like this occur in every workplace. Adam does not like coming to work and, therefore, considers it a hostile environment.

The first thing to understand about harassment is that it is not the same as bullying. Currently, there is no law against workplace bullying. Rather, the harassment must take place against a "protected class."

Under federal law, protected classes of individuals include race, color, sex, age (40 and older), religion, national origin, disability, citizenship status and genetic information. California law protects all of the same classes but also extends protection for ancestry, mental disability, medical condition, marital status, gender, gender identity, gender expression or sexual orientation or military and veteran status. Gov.C. § 12940(j)(1).

The law does not protect Adam's feelings, nor does it require that Adam and Carl be friends. The law protects groups of people whom the state of California has declared to have been marginalized by society. If Adam was Jewish and his hat was a kippah, Carl's comments could be viewed as harassment against Adam's religion.

Under the Fair Employment and Housing Act ("FEHA"), harassment can be either verbal, physical or visual. Verbal harassment includes epithets, derogatory comments or slurs (or repeated romantic overtures, sexual comments and jokes or prying into one's personal affairs). Physical harassment is any unwanted touching, rubbing against someone, assault and physical interference with movement or work. Visual harassment includes derogatory cartoons, drawings or posters or lewd gestures.

Harassment must be sufficiently "severe" or "pervasive" as to alter the conditions of employment. *Aguilar v. Avis Rent A Car System, Inc.* (1999) 21 Cal.4th 121, 130. In other words, Carl's comment about Adam's kippah must be more than just a casual comment. Occasional, isolated, sporadic or trivial acts are usually not enough to alter the conditions of employment and create a hostile work environment.

The victim of harassment must show a "concerted pattern of harassment of a repeated, routine or a generalized nature" and that the alleged conduct constituted an "unreasonably abusive or offensive work-related environment or adversely affected the reasonable employee's ability to do his or her job." *Davis v. Monsanto Chem. Co.* (6th Cir. 1988) 858 F2d 349

California requires employers to take "all reasonable steps necessary to prevent discrimination and harassment from occurring." Gov.C. § 12940(k). An employer who fails to remedy problems of which it has actual or constructive knowledge may be held liable for harassment despite the existence of a formal policy against harassment. *DeGrace v. Rumsfeld* (1st Cir. 1980) 614 F2d 796, 803.

Employers are liable for harassment by non-supervisory employees or non-employees over whom it has control (e.g., independent contractors or customers on the premises), if it knew, or should have known about the harassment and failed to take prompt and appropriate corrective action.

Such liability can be prevented by taking (and documenting) immediate action against the offending party. If the offending party is a supervisor, liability is more difficult to overcome.

An employer is <u>automatically</u> liable for harassment by a supervisor that results in a negative employment action such as termination, failure to promote or hire, and loss of wages. If the supervisor's harassment results in a hostile work environment, the employer can avoid liability only if it can prove that: 1) it reasonably tried to prevent and promptly correct the harassing behavior; and 2) the employee unreasonably failed to take advantage of any preventive or corrective opportunities provided by the employer.

While there are many forms of harassment, some are more prominent than others. Religious discrimination is actually uncommon, largely because religious beliefs are rarely expressed outwardly. A person's color and sex, on the other hand, are not so easily hid. While not every person is religious, everyone has a race and sex. That is why these forms of harassment are the most common.

Sexual Harassment

Sexual harassment has been the subject of so much litigation, it has spawned other laws. There are two forms of sexual harassment. The first is hostile work environment, which has just been discussed. The second is "quid pro quo," where an employee's subjection to sexual conduct is linked to the grant or denial of job benefits, such as getting or retaining a job, or receiving a favorable performance review or promotion.

The comment can be as innocent as an invitation to lunch or as severe as demanding sexual favors. As long as the employee was subject to unwelcome sexual advances, conduct or comments by a supervisor with authority over the employee, the employer can be held liable.

These types of claims are often "he said, she said" and are decided by the perceived truthfulness of the parties. That is not an advantageous position for an employer. California juries are comprised of the same electorate that voted for a legislature that sees corporations as an endless source of revenue.

If an employer is sued, Code of Civil Procedure § 1001 makes all confidentiality provisions in a settlement agreement void as a matter of law. This applies to all civil and administrative actions with claims related to (a) sexual assault; (b) sexual harassment; (c) workplace harassment or discrimination based on sex; (d) failure to prevent an act of workplace harassment or discrimination based on sex; (e) retaliation against a person for reporting harassment or discrimination based on sex; (f) harassment or discrimination based on sex; or (g) retaliation against a person for reporting harassment or discrimination based on sex.

Employers are encouraged to be extra diligent about preventing and investigating sexual harassment claims. Sweeping such claims under the rug will not make them go away.

Sexual Harassment Training

California law requires that all employers that have 5 or more employees must provide 1 hour of sexual harassment and abusive conduct prevention training to non-managerial employees and 2 hours of sexual harassment and abusive conduct prevention training to managerial employees once every two years.

The training must include harassment based on

gender identity, gender expression, and sexual orientation and include practical examples of such harassment and to be provided by trainers or educators with knowledge and expertise in those areas.

Employers may hire a trainer, but video trainings are also available through the Department of Fair Employment and Housing (DFEH). An employer is required to train its California-based employees so long as it employs 5 or more employees anywhere, even if they do not work at the same location and even if not all of them work or reside in California.

CHAPTER TWELVE
DISCRIMINATION

Discrimination in the hiring process has been discussed in a previous chapter and the same general legal principals of harassment apply. Discrimination must be based on a protected class (race, color, sex, age (40 and older), religion, national origin, disability, citizenship status, genetic information, ancestry, mental disability, medical condition, marital status, gender, gender identity, gender expression or sexual orientation or military and veteran status).

FEHA prohibits discrimination against the "terms, conditions, or privileges of employment" (Gov. Code § 12940(a). This is commonly referred to as a prohibition on "adverse employment action."

An adverse employment action includes, but is not limited to refusing to hire, refusing to train, discharging the employee or discriminating in compensation or terms, conditions or privileges of employment. Gov.C. § 12940(a). The adverse treatment must be "reasonably likely to impair a reasonable employee's job performance or prospects for advancement" ... as distinguished from minor or relatively trivial actions that are likely to do no more than displease. *Yanowitz v. L'Oreal USA, Inc.* (2005) 36 Cal.4th 1028, 1049.

The following provides must-know information about common forms of discrimination:

Race and National Origin Discrimination

"Race" and "color" protections are not limited to groups that traditionally have been perceived to be minorities. "Race" is interpreted broadly to mean classes of persons identifiable because of their ancestry or ethnic characteristics. *Saint Francis College v. Al-Khazraji* (1987) 481 US 604, 612-613.

"National origin" on its face means "the country where a person was born, or, more broadly, the country from which his or her ancestors came." *Espinoza v. Farah Mfg. Co., Inc.* (1973) 414 US 86, 88, 89.

There are an infinite number of ways to discriminate on the basis of race and national origin. "English-only" policies may alienate non-native employees and should not be implemented unless there is business necessity.

Dress codes may also be deemed discriminatory if they prohibit certain types of dress that are linked to certain groups. In July 2019, Governor Gavin Newsome signed the Crown Act into law, making it illegal to enforce dress code or grooming policies against hairstyles such as afros, braids, twists, and locks.

Discrimination Based on Sex

An entire book could be written on sex discrimination cases. If such a book were to be written, it would double as a detailed analysis of women's rights.

For example, in 1948, Valentine Goesaert sued under the Fourteenth Amendment's Equal Protection Clause so that women could become bartenders. *Goesart v. Cleary* (1948) 335 U.S. 464. Compare this to the 2015 case in which Ellen Pao sued after being denied promotional opportunities in the tech industry because of her sex. *Pao v. Kleiner Perkins Caufield & Byers LLC* (2015) San Francisco City and County Super. Ct. No. CGC-12-520719.

In the relatively short span of 67 years, women went from fighting for bartender jobs to fighting for partnership opportunities. This was accomplished with a case-by-case effort to establish equality in the workplace through litigation.

Despite the advancement in women's rights, discrimination still exists. That means employers should still be aware of little things that can cause liability. Stereotypes are the foundation of discrimination and should be avoided. For example, an employer should never have a policy requiring women to wear makeup. Nor should a woman be told that she cannot be a good mother while working full-time. Believe it or not, both of these were actual court cases.

The stereotyping goes both ways. In the case of *Sassaman v. Gamache* (2nd Cir. 2009) 566 F3d 307, 312, a female supervisor told a male employee who had been accused of sexual harassment that "you probably did" what complainant "said you did because you're male." The Court found that the comment about the propensity of men to sexually harass their female colleagues was evidence of sex discrimination.

"Sex" encompasses both sex (i.e., the biological differences between men and women) and gender (a person's gender-related appearance and behavior regardless of assigned sex at birth or sexual orientation).

An employer must allow an employee "to appear or dress consistently with the employee's gender identity or gender expression" Gov. Code § 12949. Employees must also be allowed to used restrooms that correspond with their gender identity or gender expression and be called by their preferred gender pronoun or name. Health & Safety Code § 118600; 2 CCR § 11034.

Age Discrimination

The first thing to understand about age discrimination is that it is not just for baby boomers. The Age Discrimination in Employment Act ("ADEA") and FEHA protect workers and job applicants over the age of 40. So, the government considers employees who rocked out to Bon Jovi and Madonna just as old as those who rocked out to Elvis and the Beatles.

The second thing to understand is how age discrimination occurs. There are a number of methods that employers might use to subtly undermine and undervalue older workers, including:

1. Demotion in favor of younger employees

2. Dismissal or "reduction in force" that has a disproportionate impact on older workers.
3. Being passed over for a promotion.
4. Harassment and unwelcome comments such as, "Hey, old timer, when are you going to retire?"
5. Favoritism and unfavorable comparisons. This could include comments or even giving better assignments to younger workers.
6. Uneven discipline

There is a four-part test that courts use to determine whether age discrimination occurred: 1) at the time of the adverse action the employee was 40 years of age or older, 2) an adverse employment action was taken against the employee, 3) at the time of the adverse action the employee was satisfactorily performing his or her job and 4) the employee was replaced in his position by a significantly younger person. *Hersant v. Cal. Dept. of Soc. Serv.* (1997) 57 Cal.App.4th 997, 1002-1003.

Courts differ on how much of an age gap between plaintiff and the workers treated more favorably is enough to infer a discriminatory intent. Some courts hold that any gap of *less than 10 years* is presumptively *insignificant,* putting the burden on plaintiff to produce evidence that the employer considered the age gap significant. *Guz v. Bechtel Nat'l, Inc.,* (2000) 24 Cal.App.4th 366, 367.

Salary is also a factor. In the case of a reduction in force, the use of salary as the basis for determining who to layoff may be found to constitute age discrimination "if use of that criterion adversely impacts older workers as a group." Gov. Code. §

12941 (emphasis added). In other words, the law recognizes that salary is reflective of experience and tenure. Therefore, cutting costs by terminating an older employee may very well be age discrimination.

Disability Discrimination

FEHA prohibits discrimination on the basis of "physical disability" or "mental disability" as defined in the Act or on the basis of any other condition covered as a "disability" under the Americans with Disabilities Act. Gov. Code § 12926(j), (l), (m), (n).

The physical or mental disability need only "limit" (not substantially limit) a major life activity. It just so happens that, under FEHA, "working" is a major life activity regardless of whether the employee cannot perform "a particular employment or a class or broad range of employments." Gov. Code § 12926.1(c).

The Legislature has stated its intent that "physical disability" be construed so that applicants and employees are protected from discrimination due to actual or perceived physical impairment that is disabling, potentially disabling, or perceived as disabling or potentially disabling. Gov. Code. § 12926.1(b).

What this means is that any type of medical condition that limits work is a disability. In recent years, the concept of "stress leave" has been the source of much litigation. In this scenario, the employee becomes so stressed by the demands of the job that it is affecting his or her mental health. The only solution is doctor-recommended time off work, which then creates a limit on a major life activity.

This triggers FEHA's requirement for employers to make "reasonable accommodation" for the known disabilities of an employee. Gov. Code. § 12940(m). This is an affirmative duty that should be carefully administered. If the employee needs a better chair, the employer must provide the chair. If the employee needs time off, the employer must provide the time off. Other accommodations could include working from home, allowing assistive animals on the worksite, modifying work schedules or department transfer.

This duty to accommodate arises even if the employee has not requested an accommodation. If the employer is aware of the disability, it has a duty to accommodate. Furthermore, the employer has a duty to "engage in the interactive process."

Pregnancy Discrimination

Pregnancy discrimination is a form of "sex" discrimination.

Unfortunately, pregnancy discrimination is a very real thing. Some employers do not want to accommodate extended leaves of absence and may attempt to discriminate against pregnant women.

In order to be liable for pregnancy discrimination, it must be shown that the employer knew she was pregnant. There must also be a "nexus" between the pregnancy and the alleged adverse employment action.

Employers also have a duty to accommodate pregnant workers. This would include severe morning sickness.

Associational Discrimination

Both the ADA and FEHA prohibit discrimination against employees who are "**associated with** a person who has, or is perceived to have, any of those characteristics." Gov. Code § 12926(o).

The courts have recognized three versions of disability-based associational discrimination, referred to as "expense," "disability by association," and "distraction." *Rope v. Auto-Chlor System of Washington, Inc.* (2013) 220 Cal.App.4th 635, 655–660.

For example, an employer may also be concerned that an employee's spouse has a disability that would be costly to the employer because the spouse is covered by the company's health plan. Even though the employer may perceive this as a purely economic decision, it is no less discriminatory.

An employer may also fear that an employee is likely to develop the disability of one of the employee's blood relatives that has a disabling ailment with a genetic component. Or the employer may fear that a homosexual employee may become infected with HIV of a companion.

Associational discrimination can also occur when an employer believes that an employee will become somewhat inattentive at work because his or her loved one has a disability that requires extra attention that will decrease the employee's productivity. The law does not permit corporate productivity to interfere with employee rights.

CHAPTER THIRTEEN
WHISTLEBLOWERS

Whistleblowing is an American past time. After all, it goes hand in hand with freedom of speech.

In 1773, Benjamin Franklin obtained the "Hutchinson Letters," which contained the opinions of a royal British governor regarding the American Colonies. The letters were published in the Boston Gazette, creating tensions that would eventually lead to the Revolutionary War.

During the Revolutionary War, the Continental Congress voted to financially support two whistleblowers, Samuel Shaw and Richard Marven, after they accused Continental Naval Officer, Esek Hopkins, of torturing British prisoners of war. This is largely regarded as the world's first whistleblower protection act.

During the Civil War, the U.S. Government passed the False Claims Act of 1863, which encouraged whistleblowing by promising a reward for information about fraud against the government. It also provided for protection against retaliation.

In 2018, the U.S. Senate unanimously passed a resolution to mark July 30th as National Whistleblower Appreciation Day to recognize whistleblowers whose actions have protected the American people from fraud or malfeasance.

However, whistleblowing has not been without its controversies. Whistleblowers against the government can be viewed as either heroes or traitors. The same feelings exist for corporate whistleblowers. The public disclosure of perceived wrongdoing can cause reputational damage to a company that ultimately results in job loss or bankruptcy.

Labor Code § 1102.5

The Merriam-Webster dictionary defines whistleblower as "an employee who brings wrongdoing by an employer or other employees to the attention of a government or law enforcement agency and who is commonly vested by statute with rights and remedies for retaliation."

California has a much broader definition of a whistleblower. Under Labor Code § 1102.5, an employer may not retaliate against an employee who disclosed, or *may* disclose, information to a government agency or any person with authority over the employee that the employee has reasonable cause to believe discloses a violation of local, state or federal law.

Labor Code § 1102.5 claims are the most commonly litigated because of its broad application. The statute became even more broad in 2015, when California made significant changes due to high-profile whistleblower news stories. The original version required making a complaint to a government agency (something employees are rarely motivated to do). The current version requires only a report to "any person with authority over the (employee)."

Whether or not there is an actual violation of law is also irrelevant. The employee is protected if he or she has "reasonable belief" that the employer's conduct is unlawful. Further, the disclosure of information does not actually have to take place. Employers are prohibited from retaliating against an employee who "may" disclose information.

Under subsection (h), the retaliatory protection extends to an employee who is a family member or the person who engaged in, or is "perceived to have engaged in," protected activity. In other words, it is possible for a former employee to file a lawsuit against a business simply by alleging that it is in retaliation for a relative that was perceived to have engaged in whistleblowing activity. These are the type of landmines being set in front of California employers.

Other Whistleblower Statutes

There are numerous whistleblower statutes. While none are as broad as the Labor Code § 1102.5, they still bring serious liability under certain circumstances.

The Sarbanes-Oxley Act prohibits an employer with publicly-traded stocks or bonds from discharging, discriminating against or retaliating against an employee for reporting employer conduct the employee "reasonably believes" violates federal securities, mail fraud, wire fraud or bank fraud laws or for assisting an SEC investigation. 18 USC § 1514A.

The Whistleblower Protection Act prohibits persons with authority over personnel actions from taking or failing to take a personnel action in retaliation for specified actions by the employee or applicant. 5 USC § 2302(b).

The Dodd-Frank Wall Street Reform and Consumer Protection Act permits the Securities and Exchange Commission to incentivize whistleblowing by paying awards to whistleblowers who provide original information about violations of the federal securities laws that lead to a successful SEC enforcement. 15 USC § 78u-6(h)(1)(A).

The Fair Labor Standards Act specifically protects employees from retaliation by employers for reporting or refusing to participate in alleged violations of Title I of the Patient Protection and Affordable Care Act. 29 USC § 218c(a)(2), (5).

The Defend Trade Secrets Act gives immunity from civil or criminal liability to whistleblowers under federal or state trade secret laws for disclosing a trade secret in confidence to a government official or an attorney "solely for the purpose of reporting or investigating a suspected violation of law." 18 USC § 1833(b).

The Energy Reorganization Act protects energy workers who report or otherwise act upon safety concerns. To establish a prima facie case of retaliation under the ERA, an employee must show that: (1) he or she engaged in a protected activity; (2)

the employer knew or suspected that the employee engaged in the protected activity; (3) the employee suffered an adverse action; and (4) the circumstances were sufficient to raise an inference that the protected activity was a contributing factor in the adverse action. 42 USC § 5851.

The aforementioned False Claims Act, first passed in 1863, is also still on the books. California has its own version of this law that establishes a cause of action for damages and penalties against persons who submit false claims for money, property or services to the State of California or political subdivisions of the state. Gov.C. §§ 12651, 12652.

Labor Code § 6310 (Cal-OSHA) prohibits employers from retaliating against employees who: (1) make oral or written complaints regarding employee safety or health to government agencies, their employer or their representative; (2) institute or testify in safety or health related proceedings; or (3) refuse to perform work in an unsafe or unhealthy environment that creates a real or apparent hazard to the employee or the employee's co-workers.

The California Fair Pay Act prohibits employers from retaliating against employees who disclose their own wages, discuss the wages of their co-workers or inquire about another employee's wages. Lab.C. § 1197.5(k)(1).

California also has industry specific statues such as Health & Safety Code § 1278.5 for health care facilities (e.g., hospitals, etc.), Gov. Code § 8547.8(c) for state employees, Gov. Code § 9149.30 for legislative employees, and Military & Veteran Code § 56 for National Guard service members.

LAND OF LIABILITY

CHAPTER FOURTEEN
WRONGFUL TERMINATION

Breaking up is hard to do. This is just as true in the employment context as it is with romance.

Just like in romantic relationship, employers demand dedication from their employees. They want exclusivity and commitment. They want loyalty. In return, employees dedicate time and energy seeking reassurance that they are performing adequately.

When the relationship ends, many employees reflect back on the relationship and wonder what they could have done better. Why was I terminated? What did I do wrong?

Absent an obvious answer, the employee turns to the possibility that the termination was wrongful. To borrow a phrase from the English playwright William Congreve, "Hell hath no fury like (an employee) scorned."

Employers need to understand that being fired is a terrible experience. Not only does it take away the employee's livelihood, but it is seen as a criticism of character. For the employer, it may be "just business." For the employee, it is a trip to the unemployment line and a permanent blemish on a resume.

When an employee views a termination as unfair and unjustified, he or she uses the synonym "wrongful." However, the term "wrongful" has a different definition in the legal context. To be a wrongful termination, it needs to be more than just unfair. The employer's conduct needs to be <u>unlawful</u>.

"At-Will" Employment
In California, all employment is presumed to be "at-will." This means that either the employer or the employee may terminate employment at any time, with or without cause or prior notice.

This is the employment equivalent of a "no-fault divorce," which was a law first passed by California stating that the dissolution of a marriage does not require a showing of wrongdoing by either party. Basically, the government does not need to be involved in the reasons for the divorce, only refereeing how everything should be divided afterward.

The employment relationship is similar. The government presumes a no-fault termination until the employee overcomes the at-will presumption by showing either 1) a breach of an employment agreement or 2) a violation of a statutory or public policy.

Beach of Employment Agreement
An employee who is terminated before the expiration of his or her contract may have grounds to

recover the full amount of that contract through a breach of contract claim. Most employment contracts define the specific reasons under which an employee may be terminated. The employer is obligated to adhere to the terms of the agreement and terminating an employee without following proper procedure may be a breach of contract.

In some cases, the employee handbook can create a binding contract. Employment contracts have not been discussed in this book because they are not recommended. The only exception would be for high-ranking managerial employees. Even then, the contract should be carefully drafted by an attorney and include provisions for terminations "for cause."

Important Public Policies

The public policy exception to at-will employment allows an employee to sue when the termination violates an important public policy. This means that an employee may sue an employer for wrongful termination if the employee was terminated for refusing to violate a law, performing a legal obligation, exercising a legal right, or reporting an alleged violation of law to the government, law enforcement or a supervisor. The most common policies that support public policy wrongful termination suits include: sexual harassment, whistleblower retaliation, and discrimination based on age, sex, disability, religion, race, and national origin. In other words, the law protects employees in a "protected class" or employees who engage in "protected activity."

Protected Class

California's "protected classes" have already been discussed in the chapters regarding harassment and discrimination. They include: sexual orientation, gender identity and gender expression, race, color, ancestry, national origin, religion, sex (including pregnancy, childbirth, and related medical conditions), medical conditions, AIDS/HIV, disability (physical or mental), age (40 and older), genetic information, marital status, military or veteran status, political affiliations or activities, and status as a victim of domestic violence, assault, or stalking.

If termination arises because an employee is part of one of these protected classes, then the termination may be wrongful. Remember, it is not enough to be a member of a protected class. There must be nexus between the termination and the discrimination.

Protected Activity

Wrongful termination or retaliation may also be present if the employee was engaged in "protected activity." There is no set definition of protected activity. The activities are set by statute and cover a wide-range of issues. The Department of Industrial Relations lists 47 actionable statutes under the Labor Code, including:

- Retaliating against an employee for lawful conduct outside of work. Labor Code § 96(k)
- Retaliating against an employee for filing or threatening to file a claim or complaint with the Labor Commissioner. Labor Code § 98.6
- Retaliating against an employee for taking

time off to serve on a jury. Labor Code § 230(a))
- Retaliating against an employee for being a victim of a crime and testifying as witness to a judicial proceeding. Labor Code § 230(b)
- Retaliating against an employee for being a victim of domestic violence, sexual assault, and/or stalking. Labor Code §§ 230(c), (e), (f); 230.1; 230.2(b)
- Retaliating against an employee for taking time off to be a volunteer firefighter or reserve peace officer, or an officer. Labor Code §§ 230.3, 230.4
- Retaliating against an employee for taking time off to appear at a child's school. Labor Code §§ 230.7; 230.8 and Education Code § 48900.1
- Requiring an employee to refrain from disclosing or discussing the amount of his or her wages. Labor Code §s 232(a) and (b)
- Requiring an employee to refrain from disclosing or discussing information about the employer's working conditions. Labor Code § 232.5
- Retaliating against an employee for using or attempting to use sick leave. Labor Code §§ 233, 234, 245-249
- Reporting or threatening to report the citizenship or immigration status of an employee, former employee or prospective employee. Labor Code § 244
- Relying on an applicant's salary history as a factor in determining whether to offer

employment to the applicant and at what salary to make an offer to the applicant. Labor Code § 432.3
- Requiring disclosure of information concerning an arrest or detention that did not result in conviction. Labor Code § 432.7
- Requiring disclosure of information regarding a conviction related to the possession of marijuana where the conviction is more than two years old. Labor Code § 432.8
- Using a consumer credit report for employment purposes unless the position of the person for whom the report is sought is any of the enumerated exemptions. Labor Code § 1024.5
- Refusing to provide reasonable accommodations for an employee to participate in an alcohol or drug rehabilitation program. Labor Code §§ 1025-1028
- Retaliation against an employee who requests a lactation accommodation or who attempts to express breast milk. Labor Code §§ 1030-1033
- Refusing to assist an employee in an adult literacy education program. Labor Code § 1041-1044
- Retaliating against or attempting to assert control over an employee who participates in politics or who become candidates for public office. Labor Code § 1101
- Coercing, influencing or attempting to coerce

or influence an employees' political activity. Labor Code § 1102
- Retaliation for whistleblower activity. Labor Code § 1102.5
- Interfering with participation in a national service program (e.g., AmeriCorps). Labor Code § 1171
- Paying an employee less than the opposite sex. Labor Code § 1197.5
- Retaliating against an employee who refuses to work hours in excess of those permitted by the Industrial Welfare Commission (IWC) Orders. Labor Code § 1198.3
- Retaliating against an employee who exercises the right to take a paid leave of absence for the purpose of donating his or her organ or bone marrow to another person. Labor Code § 1512
- Using E-Verify to check the employment authorization status of an existing employee or applicant who has not been offered employment at a time or in a manner not required by federal law, authorized by a federal agency, or as a condition of receiving federal funds. Labor Code § 2814
- Discrimination against an employee whose wages have been subjected to garnishment. Labor Code § 2929(b) and (c)
- Failing to provide an employee with a "mystery shopper" report before terminating the employee. Labor Code § 2930
- Retaliating against an employee who complains about safety or health conditions

or practices. Labor Code § 6310
- Retaliating against an employee who refuses to perform work that violates health and safety. Labor Code § 6311
- Retaliating against an employee who refuses to lift, reposition, or transfer a patient due to the health care worker's concerns about patient or worker safety or because of the lack of trained lift team personnel or equipment. Labor Code § 6403.5
- Retaliating against an employee who expresses an opinion concerning an alternative workweek election or for opposing or supporting its adoption or repeal. IWC Orders 1 through 13, § 3(C)(8); IWC Order 16, § 3(C)(7); and IWC Order 17, § 5 "Election Procedures" (H)

The Balancing Test

Wrongful termination, retaliation or discrimination are subject to a balancing test known as the *McDonnel Douglas* test.

Under the *McDonnell Douglas* test, the employee has the initial burden of establishing a prima facie case of discrimination by showing that it is more likely than not that such actions were "based on a [prohibited] discriminatory criterion…"

If the employee can establish a prima facie case, then a presumption of discrimination arises, and the burden shifts to the employer to rebut the presumption by producing evidence sufficient to raise a genuine issue of material fact the employer took its actions for a legitimate, nondiscriminatory reason. The burden then shifts back to the employee to prove that there was discriminatory intent.

The purpose of the *McDonnel Douglas* test is to allow the employer an opportunity to maintain some control over their business. Employers are not required to forever employ workers of a protected class for fear of a lawsuit. If the workers are underperforming in their job duties, then there is a legitimate business reason for the termination.

Note that this balancing test was not implemented by the California legislature. The *McDonnel Douglas* test was mandated by the U.S. Supreme Court in 1973 while deciding a case under the Civil Rights Act of 1964. Shortly thereafter, it was adopted by the California courts. The most important defense for employers, which brings an element of fairness to court proceedings, was not created by elected California officials.

Documents Required to be Given to Terminated Employees

After the decision has been made to terminate an employee, there are certain legal requirements that must be met. For example, federal law requires that all employers with 20 or more employees provide a Consolidated Omnibus Budget Reconciliation Act (COBRA) notice and election form to employees who are participating in the employer's group health plan the day before the termination and to any of the terminating employee's dependents on the plan. Cal-COBRA must be offered to both terminated employees of small employers (2-19 employees) and terminated employees covered under federal

COBRA when their 18 months of federal COBRA coverage expires.

No later than the effective date of the discharge or layoff, all discharged or laid off employees must receive a pamphlet from the California Employment Development Department (EDD) entitled "For Your Benefit" (DE 2320). California Unemployment Insurance Code 1089 requires employers to give a written Notice to Employee as to Change in Relationship form to all discharged or laid off employees immediately upon termination. No written notice is required if it is a voluntary quit, promotion or demotion, change in work assignment or location or if work stopped due to a trade dispute.

The Department of Health Care Services requires employers with 20 or more employees to provide the Health Insurance Premium Payment (HIPP) notice, DHCS 9061, to certain employees covered under the program.

California Labor Code § 2808(b) requires employers to provide to employees, upon termination, notification of all continuation, disability extension and conversion coverage options under any employer-sponsored coverage for which the employee may remain eligible after employment terminates.

If an employer intends to lay off 50 or more employees, a WARN Act notice must be sent out 60 days prior to termination. The Internal Revenue Service (IRS) may also require notices to terminating employees within certain time frames to advise them of their rights to retirement benefits. If retirement benefits are applicable, seek guidance from the IRS.

Notifying the Employee

Notifying an employee of termination is never an easy task. However, there are some ways to make the notification process easier.

First, plan a meeting during work hours with the employee. At the meeting, the manager should provide a short explanation for the decision. This is not the time to delve into the employee's employment history or negotiate extending the working relationship. Remember, employers are not required to provide an explanation for their decision to at-will employees. It is strongly recommended that this portion of the meeting be kept short with as little information offered as possible. Disgruntled employees and clever attorneys can easily misconstrue such statements.

The meeting should also include information on the employee's final pay and benefit information, including COBRA. Have the employee sign all necessary documents and provide the required documents mentioned previously in this letter. Obtain any company property from the individual.

Discuss any severance offer and provide a separation agreement, which should contain a release of claims. Seek the advice of an attorney in drafting this important legal document. Let the employee know that they are free to sign the agreement in your presence or take it home to review. Do not go into detail about the terms of the agreement, other than the amount.

If the individual responds with anger, the manager should stay calm, give the employee time to vent, and then repeat the employer's message. Show compassion and understanding for someone who responds emotionally to the news but return to the company message.

Other employees will certainly want to know about the termination(s). It is important to provide a truthful explanation while maintaining privacy of the employee. Simply explain to current employees about how job duties are going to be divided up. Provide customers with reassurances that their needs will still be met. Once again, do not share details of the decision or disparage the former employee in any way.

CHAPTER FIFTEEN
LITIGATION

In 2017, specialty insurer Hiscox performed a survey and found that US companies had at least a 10.5% chance of having an employment charge filed against them. Unsurprisingly, California employers were 40% more likely to receive a charge than employers in other states.

While the purpose of this book is to help California employers avoid litigation, the reality is that allegations are always lurking. Here is some practical advice about what to do after being served with a lawsuit.

1. Stay Calm but Have a Sense of Urgency. A defendant has 30 days after the date of service to file a response with the court. The 30 days include weekend days and court holidays. Time can go by quickly, so there should be a sense of urgency. Employers should read the Complaint and determine the nature of the case. It may be a recent event or something that happened three or four years ago. As

much information as possible should be recalled.
2. Preserve Records. Next, try to locate documents related to the lawsuit and store them in a safe place. If possible, electronic copies should be made. In California, litigants owe an "uncompromising duty to preserve" what they know or reasonably should know will be relevant evidence in a pending lawsuit. Litigation can take years to complete and it is much easier to preserve evidence early. It is also a good idea to record the names and contact information of relevant witnesses.
3. Consult an Attorney. A corporation cannot be represented by a non-attorney, so an attorney should be consulted as soon as possible. Most law firms offer free consultations, so any advice will be worth the price. An experienced attorney will be able to spot key defenses or any procedural defects in the complaint. Be upfront and tell your attorney everything. The truth will come out eventually and it is better to know the potential liability early on.
4. Carry On. One of the benefits of retaining an attorney is the ability to share the burden. Your attorney will worry about deadlines and appearances, so you can focus on your business. Litigation takes time and, in full honesty, money. But don't run out and file for bankruptcy just because you're in a lawsuit. A strong defense can decrease liability. You

retain an attorney to defend your interests and a good attorney will do just that.

Defense of a lawsuit starts <u>before</u> the lawsuit is filed. That is the best advice for any California employer and the reason why this book was written. Here are some tips for preventing employment-related lawsuits:

1. Knowledge. Ignorance of the law is the number one reason businesses get sued. "We didn't know," is not a defense. Employers must know California law.
2. Recordkeeping. As previously discussed, maintaining records can be a legal requirement. However, it is good business practice to make and keep employee files.
3. Policies. Employment policies need to be created and <u>followed</u>. Management, employees and lawyers will refer to the employee handbook when disputes arise.
4. Investigate and Resolve. Never sleep on a problem. If a whistleblower comes forward, deal with the subject of the complaint and <u>not the employee</u>. Whistleblowers can be assets by alerting employers to potential liability. Many employees prefer to make complaints in-house. However, if the employee fears retaliation or does not have trust in the employer's reporting process, they will report the information to an outside source such as the government or media. If that happens, the employer does not have an opportunity to resolve the issue.

Being sued often triggers the five steps of grief

and loss – Denial, Anger, Bargaining, Depression and Acceptance.

Denial usually comes in the form of declaring the lawsuit "frivolous." Under Code of Civil Procedure § 128.5, "Frivolous means totally and completely without merit or for the sole purpose of harassing an opposing party." As long as there is some merit to the claim, no matter how small, it will not be found frivolous. That is why, out of the 480,506 civil cases filed in 2015, only five were found to be frivolous under Code of Civil Procedure § 128.5.

Denial is overcome when there appears to be an element of truth, or at least a disputable issue of fact. That is when anger spawns the question, "How could this have happened?" Blame is directed at anyone involved, including supervisors and employees.

At some point, the parties are going to attempt settlement. 98% of civil cases settle and the court makes settlement discussions mandatory. During the settlement process, each side takes turns pointing out weak arguments and making counterpoints. The employer may even need to engage in internal bargaining in order to offer money for a settlement.

At some point, the employer arrives at acceptance. Usually this comes in the form of a business decision. It is very expensive to defend a case through trial. It would be even more expensive to go to trial and lose. Under most circumstances, the employer makes a determination that it would be cheaper to settle than pursue a trial and lose. That decision, however, should be made with advice from a qualified employment law attorney.

There is no winning a lawsuit. The process takes

years to complete and legal fees can be expensive. Corporations must be represented by a licensed attorney so there is no avoiding the legal costs. Therefore employers should implement solid employment practices aimed at avoiding liability.

ABOUT THE AUTHOR

Daniel Thompson is an employment law and business litigation attorney with jury trial experience. His academic accolades include a Juris Doctor from Western Sierra Law School and an LL.M. in Public Law and Policy from the University of the Pacific McGeorge School of Law.

As one of eight children born to a small business owner, Mr. Thompson understands the struggles of small and family-owned businesses. Growing up in Fallbrook, Mr. Thompson experienced first-hand the growth of business in Temecula and the surrounding areas. His familiarity with government and business is what inspired him to become a business lawyer.

In July 2019, Mr. Thompson was named one of the "Top 100 Attorneys" in the area of employment law by the American Academy of Attorneys. As a Temecula employment lawyer, Mr. Thompson has an impressive track record of litigating wrongful termination and discrimination claims, earning millions for his clients. Other areas of expertise include retaliation, harassment, unpaid wages and meal and rest period violations.

Mr. Thompson has quickly gained a reputation as a proficient leader in the field of employment law and maintains a blog dedicated to subject. The blog articles and related videos discuss current issues involving the employment relationship with the purpose of educating both employers and employees on the requirements of California law. Interested readers can locate the blog at southerncaliforniaemploymentlaw.com.

In addition to litigation, Mr. Thompson offers a wide range of business services directed at ensuring that his business clients are compliant with state and federal law. These services include drafting employee handbooks and contracts, presenting employee trainings, participating in alternative dispute resolution, and conducting workplace investigations.

During his legal carrier, Mr. Thompson has represented corporations, public entities, and individuals throughout California, including Riverside, San Diego, Orange, Los Angeles, Ventura and San Bernardino counties. Mr. Thompson has litigated cases in the federal and state court and has found success in front of a jury.

Mr. Thompson is also an accomplished author and publisher. In 2013, he published "Peter Pomperfield and the Battle for Grandma's House," which was followed by two sequels, "Siege of Fair Oak Elementary" and "War for Camp Willalacky." In addition, Mr. Thompson has republished many books that were seemingly lost to history, including two books written by his great grandfathers in the 1800's. He remains a dedicated author and plans to publish more books in the future.

www.ingramcontent.com/pod-product-compliance
Lightning Source LLC
Chambersburg PA
CBHW071419210526
45465CB00001B/459